THE PUBS

OF

BARNES, EAST SHEEN AND MORTLAKE

by

Alan Bushell

c 2002 Barnes and Mortlake History Society

First published in 2002

by Barnes and Mortlake History Society

ISBN   0 - 9542036 - 0 - 1

Printed and bound in the United Kingdom

CONTENTS

Acknowledgements	5
Introduction	7
The Evolution of Public Houses	9
Present Pubs	
Barnes	15
East Sheen	50
Mortlake	61
Past Pubs	
Barnes	75
East Sheen	95
Mortlake	114
Inn Signs Past and Present	144
Tokens	156
Glossary	159
References	163
Index	166

Acknowledgements

Because much of the truth about the history of ale-houses, inns and taverns has been varied and embellished while being handed down through generations, often over a pint of ale or beer, many sources have been used in an attempt to compile a complete and accurate picture of those public houses mentioned in this book.

The author's best thanks are due to the following for their help in the preparation of this book.

The staffs of the City of Westminster Archives Centre; the Greater London Record Office; the Guildhall Library; the Local Studies Room at Richmond Old Town Hall; the Surrey Record Office; the Church Commissioners; the Company of Watermen and Lightermen; the Worshipful Company of Butchers; the Company of Brewers; the Brewers Society; the National Army Museum; the Public Record Office; Greene King Plc; Hall & Woodhouse Limited; Scottish & Newcastle Retail, Southern Inns Limited.

The following Company Archivists:- Mr Ken Thomas - Courage Limited; Mr N B Redman - Whitbread Plc; Mrs Helen Osborn - Young & Co's Brewery Plc.

The following members of the Barnes and Mortlake History Society:- Mrs Maisie Brown, Mr Graeme Cruickshank, Mr Nicholas Dakin, the late Mr Leslie Freeman, Miss Mary Grimwade, the late Mr Charles Hailstone, Mr Ron Knight, and Mr Brian Hunter.

Information on the Two Brewers supplied by Mr John Gibbon, and on Hawkes and Company supplied by Mr Ian Stratford. Hawkes & Company public house photographs by Simpson Brothers of Cambridge 1879.

The Barnes and Mortlake History Society gratefully acknowledges the generous donation from Young & Co Brewers Plc and financial support from two members of the society

Introduction

A walk around Barnes, East Sheen and Mortlake will tell you that there are seventeen public houses, many of which are long established and continue to play an important role in local social life, but hidden in the mists of time are many more inns, taverns and ale houses of Barnes, East Sheen and Mortlake past.

Some such as The Beare, known to have been in Barnes in the seventeenth century, The Princess Arms and The Maidenhead, in Mortlake in the seventeenth century, and The Dogge at East Sheen which went back even further in time, are known only as names mentioned in local records; their former locations have yet to be discovered.

Along with the Church, the public house was often the centre of the community both figuratively and literally, and many early village meetings were held there. Decisions that affected the growth of Barnes, East Sheen and Mortlake were made in public houses such as The Sun at Barnes when vestry meetings adjourned from St Mary's Church. The Kings Arms at Mortlake and The Hare and Hounds at East Sheen were often used for the sessions of various courts of the Lord of the Manor, whilst The Bull at Shene was used by Barnes Borough Council to hold their Council meetings.

The public house acted as village hall, town council chamber and court room, as well as the centre for fun, frivolity and relaxation. It also served as a games room, newsagents, post office, betting shop and sports centre.

So pour yourself a glass of your favourite tipple and sit back and enjoy a historical tour round the Barnes, East Sheen and Mortlake public houses – past and present.

The Evolution of the Public House

When we consider the history of the ale houses, beer houses and taverns of Barnes, East Sheen and Mortlake it is necessary to spend some time explaining their background. No doubt from very early days intoxicating liquors of one sort or another would have formed part of the daily life of the Barnes, East Sheen and Mortlake communities.

In Saxon and Mediaeval days the larger religious houses during the tenth century were the undisputed leaders when it came to matters of hospitality. Accommodation was set aside in their buildings for the few travellers, mostly merchants, traders and pilgrims, who would receive a welcome according to their status. Each religious establishment made its own rules according to its resources but in many cases it seems that it was obligatory for them to provide travellers with suitable accommodation for up to two days and two nights. The local church often had a guest house or inn for these travellers. Hence the proximity of many inns to the village church and also of inns which have at least a religious connotation.

Some of the thorns in the side of both church and state during this time were celebrations known as ales - merry gatherings variously combined with usually self - explanatory prefixes such as ale-silver, bede-ale, bride-ale, Christmas-ale, church-ale, a periodic festival gathering for the purpose of raising money for the parish church. The ale for this occasion was usually a superior brew which had been brewed in the church house from malt either bought or begged by the church wardens. Easter-ale, scot-ale, whitsun-ale, and so on. These celebrations were functions at which ale was the predominant refreshment and frequently degenerated into occasions where the behaviour of the participants was unseemly! They were clearly a blight upon the period and we find that the church forbade their priests to organise them or to take part. It was not until the seventeenth century that they were brought under satisfactory control. There are no records of church ales in Barnes, East Sheen or Mortlake as the custom had died out before the earliest church records, but it is likely that the events took place here as elsewhere.

Towards the end of the thirteenth century a new civic post was created and known as the ale taster except in London where he was described as the ale conner. The main task of the ale taster or ale conner was to assess the quality of the ale offered for sale. Without the benefit of measuring instruments this was not an easy task and one which required some skill in addition, no doubt, to a strong head! The ale taster or ale conner was required to visit the brewers before the brew was allowed to be released to the consumer, and it had to be checked that the brew was of the correct quality and matched the price permitted by the Assize. The ale taster or ale conner was vested with the authority to downgrade an ale in price if he was of the opinion that it did not represent correct value for money.

It seems that retailers of ale did not represent the most law - abiding section of the community, as this is amply testified by the records of court proceedings over a wide area during this period.

The predominant offences concerned firstly the selling of ale in unstamped measures and secondly brewers who failed to put ale stakes in front of their houses to denote that the ale taster or ale conner was required to pass a new brew fit for sale. There are no records of court proceedings for offenders in Barnes, East Sheen or Mortlake selling ale in unstamped measures or failing to put the ale stake in front of their house.

Little was known of the numerical spread of the three main types of retailing establishment until July 1577, when an Order of Council was made for a return to be prepared of the exact number of ale houses, taverns and inns in England and Wales – as yet the English Government had no jurisdiction over Scotland. The purpose of this census was to raise a levy to help towards the cost of repairing Dover Harbour. Their numbers totalled 19,759. About 88% were ale houses. 10% were inns and 2% were taverns. If it is accepted that the population of England and Wales was about 3,700,000 at that time, then there was one retail outlet for every 187 people.

The return for the County of Surrey (excluding Southwark) shows that there were 369 ale houses, 77 inns and only 8 taverns, (PRO: SP 12/17 no 301 and SP 12/96 p 408). Whilst both these documents give the total for the County, neither gives separate figures for Barnes, East Sheen or Mortlake or for anywhere else within the County.

Ale houses were sometimes called tippling houses, where beer and ale were `brewed and sold on the premises. Ale was the more ancient of the drinks – beer, which included hops, had been introduced from Flanders c 1400. Taverns were premises where wine along with ale and beer could be sold, whilst the inn provided shelter, stabling etc. as well as food and drink.

John Taylor (1580 – 1653) a Thames waterman, poet, politician and publican compiled a Catalogue of Taverns in Ten Shires around London in 1636. He mentions a tavern in Barnes kept by Richard Hill and known by the sign of The Beare. There is no public house by that name in Barnes today and where it was situated has yet to be discovered. He also mentions two taverns in Mortlake one kept by Mike Bourne (a name found in the Mortlake Vestry Minute Books) and known by the sign of The Princess Arms. The other kept by Phoebe Tucker was known by the sign of The Maidenhead. There are no public houses by these names in Mortlake today and where they were located, presumably close to the river bank, has yet to be determined.

Ale houses were licensed by the Justices of the Peace and the landlord had to find recognizances of his character, and it is from these records that part of our knowledge of the early Barnes, East Sheen and Mortlake ale houses is derived. One of the odd things about the records which do exist is that the recognizances appear to have been given by other licensed victuallers in the area. The ale house was essentially the poor man's club and meeting place. The Justices of the Peace kept as tight a hold over it as they could and it was closely watched by the village constables. The licensee was supposed to close his house early, to shut on Sunday and not allow customers to stay drinking for longer than an hour, to prohibit dicing or gambling, to keep out undesirables, to ensure the ale was of good quality and sold for a fixed price. The usual price of best ale in the seventeenth century was a penny a quart, so it was possible to get drunk for two pence. Spirits, such as gin, did not come within the reach of ordinary people until the eighteenth century, so ale was virtually a necessity of life, and variety was lent to it by spicing, warming or sweetening.

In 1659 we find Peter Issenburg of Mortlake being licensed to keep a common victualling house in the place where he dwelt, for one year following. Despite being licensed, innkeepers still managed to get into trouble for keeping disorderly houses. We find Robert Burges of Barnes kept ill rule and allowed the evil disposed to drink to get drunk, giving a bad example. John Williams kept a disorderly house during divine service on 3 July 1664. Where in Barnes these houses were situated has yet to be discovered. June Scryver of Mortlake kept inmates in her house in Mortlake and was fined for it. We are not told what sort of inmates they were but are left to guess, or where the disorderly house was situated.

An abstract of a particular account of all the inns and ale houses in England with the stable room and bedding for guests (1668) [PRO: WO 30.48] mentions Barnes 9 beds 6 stabling. This could possibly be a reference to The Beare.

In 1688 there were seventeen ale houses out of 186 rated houses in Mortlake. Where these ale houses were situated has yet to be discovered. It is possible that they were mainly located near to the river.

By the turn of the eighteenth century the coaching era was underway, and inns became important stopping points for not only the travellers to obtain food and lodging but also for the essential change of horses. The standards went up to cater for this new trade, and at the same time ale houses began to improve their facilities to counteract the demand for cheap gin which was by now becoming something of a problem.

The next boost to the brewery trade was in 1780 when a tax on malt was introduced. This tax was as great for private individual brewers as it was for the large commercial brewer. This meant that the owner of an ale house found it uneconomical to brew his own beer and consequently had to depend on the commercial brewer for his supplies. We encounter the effect of this tax in Barnes when John Waring began supplying beer to a number of the local hostelries in the early 1800's, whilst Fuller Smith and Turner had a leasehold interest in The Kings Arms in Mortlake.

However, the most cataclysmic change to the industry came in 1830 when the Duke of Wellington introduced his Sale of Beer Act which was intended to encourage beer drinking in the face of the over-consumption of cheap spirits. Any household paying rates to the parish could open a beer shop on the payment of two guineas and there was no question of a character qualification. It is around this time that several of the Barnes, East Sheen and Mortlake public houses were established.

The coming of the railway in 1846, appears to have had little effect on the Barnes public houses as the station is located well away from the village, however as the station for East Sheen and Mortlake is located closer to both communities the clientele of the East Sheen and Mortlake public houses may well have changed as the railway brought greater numbers of people to the area.

The twentieth century continued to see further changes in the Barnes, East Sheen and Mortlake public houses: from the domination of the big breweries to the Campaign for Real Ale, to the spread of multiples, or chains, to theme pubs, and all day opening. But despite all of this, some of the Barnes, East Sheen and Mortlake public houses manage to retain a timeless charm.

Present Pubs

Map of Barnes showing the location of the present public houses

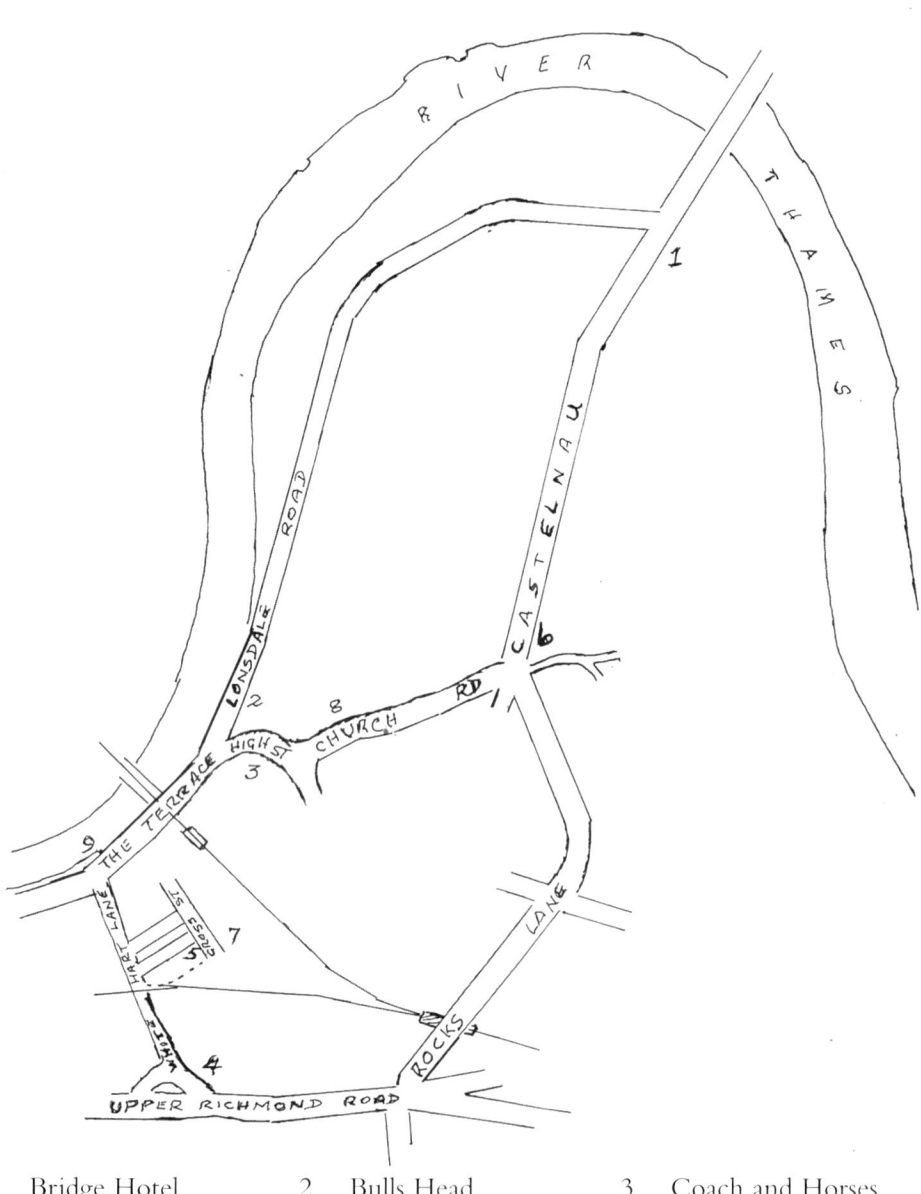

1	Bridge Hotel	2	Bulls Head	3	Coach and Horses
4	Halfway House	5	Manor Arms	6	Red Lion
7	Rose of Denmark	8	Sun Inn	9	Ye White Hart Hotel

Barnes – SW 13

The Bridge Hotel   204 Castelnau

The earliest record of this public house on the opposite side of Castelnau from The Boileau Arms dates from 1866.

Landlords

1866 - 1882 Gilbert Wardell   22 March 1911 Henry Coates

An agreement dated 25 March 1916 exists between Watney, Combe, Reid & Co. Ltd★ and a Mrs Edith Williams granting her a 10 - year lease of the premises:

> *"All that piece of land or ground situate in Upper Bridge Road, Castelnau, Barnes in the County of Surrey, together with the messuage, tenement and public house erected on part thereof and known as The Bridge Hotel and out offices, stablings and erections belonging thereto".*

For all this Mrs Williams, wife of Henry Williams, was required to pay an annual rent of £80.

In the 1920's and 1930's the licensing hours were half an hour later on the Surrey side of Hammersmith Bridge. It was quite usual at 10.00pm to see men come from the Hammersmith public houses, pay 1d fare to Barnes and go into the Bridge Hotel until 10.30 pm.

Landlords:-   1939   Mr Percy Williams
               1960   D Williams

The Bridge Hotel in 1999 was owned by Scottish and Newcastle Retail.

★*The registered office of Watney Combe Reid & Co. Ltd was at that time The Stag Brewery, Pimlico in the County of Middlesex.*

Barnes Mortlake and Sheen Times
Friday May 17 1996

The Bulls Head   373 Lonsdale Road

The Ash family are first mentioned in 1670, and from 9 July 1737 held one messuage and wharf, in the tenure of Mr Henry Barr, near wharf of Mr John Emberton: another messuage formerly The Kings Head now The Bulls Head in tenure of Mr John Smith (1737 – 1742) and a store house in the tenure of Mr James Singer: was held by Mrs Margaret Yates (formerly Ash). On Tuesday 23 June 1747 the above mentioned messuage was passed by Mrs Margaret Yates to her niece and heir Letitia Yates. Letitia and her husband William, a gardener from Richmond, surrendered out of court on 9 June 1748 this messuage to William Watson of Putney, a brewer, who was admitted to the property on 25 June 1748.

The messuages in Barnes held by William Watson then passed to Paul Watson his youngest son and heir on Saturday 26 June 1753. As Paul Watson was, at that time, an infant, his mother Jane Watson had charge of him and of the land. Namely one messuage and wharf, near wharf of Mr John Emberton, now in the tenure of Mr Thomas Barr, late Mr Henry Barr; another The Bulls Head late The Kings Head now in the tenure of Mr John Robinson, late Mr John Smith, store house in the tenure of Mr Edmund Singer, late Mr James Singer: cottage adjoining messuage in the tenure of Mr Thomas Barr.

On 26 January 1766 control of The Bulls Head passed to another brewer, Mr Henry Hunt. Mrs Elizabeth Hunt inherited her husband's properties and controlled much of the hop growing, malting, brewing and sale of beer in Barnes. Their daughter, Frances, married John Waring, a surgeon of St Thomas Hospital.

The Barnes Vestry Minutes dated 13 October 1777 recorded that the Vestry summoned a general meeting of the inhabitants of Barnes at The Bulls Head to discuss plans with regard to the building of a New Workhouse. Eighteen people attended. Meetings presumably continued here until about November 1778 when the building of the Workhouse was completed and fitting out and furnishing was commenced.

From the Land Tax Records in conjunction with the Licensed Victuallers Recognizances it has been possible to trace the landlords of The Bulls Head back to the year 1780 – 1784 when the name of Preston is recorded as the licensee. Between 1785 – 1792 the licensee was Mrs Elizabeth Preston, she was succeeded in 1793 by Mr John Bailey who remained there until 1799, when his widow Mrs Elizabeth Bailey took over for a year. In 1801 Mr John Cook was the licensee until he was succeeded in 1803 by Mr Robert Elliot who remained there until 1817.

The Barnes Churchwardens' accounts for the year 1808 record that Mr Robert Elliot was paid five shillings and five pence for a visitation dinner and also ten shillings and ten pence for a perambulation dinner. This clearly shows that The Bulls Head was serving food as well as drink in the early nineteenth century.

A visitation was usually an official visit, by a high member of the church to inspect the Parish Accounts or alternatively a visit to sort out trouble or difficulty regarding a divine punishment.

Perambulation means to walk, it was the custom in Ascension week to walk and define the boundaries of the Parish. The ceremony was carried out by the Incumbent, church wardens and parishioners, and a dinner was often provided after the perambulation.

Sometime during the year of 1817 Mr Elliot was succeeded by Mr John Hall. In 1821 Mrs Sarah Warren was the licensee and when she left in 1828 she kept a small chandlers shop on the other side of the High Street.

At that time there was a long room detached from the house by a yard, and there was also a skittle alley, with a fine vine growing overhead.

The trade of The Bulls Head, however was intimately connected with the activities of the river by reason of its position and because of the landing stage which was part of the same messuage. A drawing in 1826 shows the numerous boats and busy activity at the wharf which no doubt brought much trade to The Bulls Head. Many of the provisions were still brought by river in the 1870's. Mr John Cook who made tobacco pipes in Malthouse Passage and kept two horses and carts to distribute clay pipes to publicans, had clay sent to him in barges which came up to this wharf. After work, the barge men and the local inhabitants could relax at The Bulls Head.

The licensee between 1829 - 1831 was Mr William Walker and he was succeeded by Mr James Thornton 1832 - 1847, or Jimmy Thornton as he was called, who had previously been the licensee at Ye White Hart Hotel.

As a Queen's messenger, and property owner, Mr John Waring had the present building constructed in 1845 and today it towers over the adjacent Watermans Arms (see Barnes past pubs) in Hapsburgian splendour. John Waring owned the nearby wharf and cottage which was then part of The Bulls Head. At that time the owner of the next door cottage who had a blacksmiths forge adjoining, was frustrated in the hope that Waring would give him a good price for the forge. Out of spite, when his hopes were dashed, he built The Watermans Arms alongside.

On the death of Mr John Waring in 1865, his properties passed to his daughter, Mary Catherine Waring who had made a good marriage to Major General Arthur Stevens. On 27 July 1871, Mary Waring let The Bulls Head to Mr Charles Florence Young and Anthony Fothergil Bainbridge, common brewers, and the records from then onwards refer to Charles Florence Young as the Owner.

Other licensees have been Mr John Hulbert 1851, Mr Henry Pankhurst 1860 - 1878, Mr

The Bulls Head - Barnes - c 1900-03

William Tooley 1880, and Mr William Looke Smith 1882 - 1896.

The Bulls Head was enfranchised by Edwin Richardson Goolden in 1896 and at that time comprised that messuage or tenement called or known by the name of The Bulls Head as the same is situated adjoining The Watermans Arms and facing the river Thames and is now or late was in the tenure or occupation of W L Smith together with the premises in rear consisting of stabling, coach house, sheds, and yard.

Landlords:-   Mr George Garrett 1900 - 1903 and Mr Charles H Cates 1939.

Visitors to The Bulls Head were amazed during the week commencing November 1972 when they were charged 1957 prices for their drinks. A pint of beer was on offer for 10 pence (old money) as was a glass of scotch or gin, much to the delight of all and sundry. It was all in aid of landlord Mr Albert Tolley's twentieth anniversary at The Bulls Head, which he personally has made famous throughout the world for its jazz music.

Years of experience in running public houses and a lifetime's love of jazz music made Dan and Liz Fleming jump at the chance of running Barnes' famous jazz public house in 1981. The spacious main bar and carvery of The Bulls Head overlook the river, "Its such a beautiful spot" said Dan, "it attracts lots of people and its all hands to the pumps on Boat Race Day."

All the food is made on the premises. The carvery serves roasts, pies and sandwiches every day, and the Flemings also run The Stable Bistro in the old stable behind the public house. This has a more elaborate choice of food, here too all freshly made to order, and overflows into the courtyard in summer. The Stable Bistro (June 1988) was only open on Thursday, Friday and Saturday evenings, because demand had dropped with the closure of Hammersmith Bridge.

Jazz performances have been held in a separate room every night since 1959, and twice on Sundays. Great performers come from all over Europe, the United States and even the Antipodes to this famous venue, and Dan still finds time to put together the programme and publicise it every month. Fans come from all over London to Barnes' own local jazz institution.

At 8 pm on Thursday 14 April 1983 The Bulls Head regulars, the Tony Lee Trio, provided the jazz in the first of four stints during the week, and were joined by Nigel Nash and Dick Pearce. On Saturday evening they teamed up with Stan Robinson and Dave Quincey. The Sunday lunchtime session saw them appear with Tommy Whittle and Martin Drew on drums, while in the evening they were partnered by Tommy Whittle and Terry Smith.

Friday night's spot was filled by the Phil Bates Trio who were joined by Ted Beament, Don Wheller and Dick Morrissey. The Monday night music was provided by Paz - Ray Warleigh, Geoff Castle, Frank Ricotti and Glen Cartlidge. The Bill le Sage, Art Themen Quartet appeared on Tuesday, whilst the Wednesday night was a bit special with the Humphrey Lyttleton Band,

The Bulls Head - c 1920 - Rebuilt in 1847, formerly the Kings Head in 1737, The Watermans Arms built c 1850 on the site of a blacksmiths forge.

The Bulls Head and the police station - c 1960 - Lonsdale Road

featuring Bruce Turner and Mike Pyne.

At the end of November 1985 a three week jazz festival was staged by The Greater London Arts in association with the Musicians' Union to celebrate 25 years of jazz at The Bulls Head. Big names from the jazz world – included John Dankworth, Humphrey Lyttleton, Stan Tracy, Ronnie Scott and Georgie Fame – all made appearances.

The Bulls Head and Watermans Arms - Barnes - c 1960 - The junction of the High Street with Lonsdale Road and The Terrace.

The Coach and Horses   27 Barnes High Street

The Coach and Horses is an amalgam of styles, strategically located to welcome traders today as it welcomed travellers to and from London in the eighteenth and nineteenth centuries. A pleasant white painted building, it has a garden at the rear and a long room now used for storage which was formerly a skittle alley.

The Barnes Churchwardens' accounts of October 1776 refer to beer from The Coach and Horses, 8d. Unfortunately they do not give any indication of the volume supplied for this sum. No doubt it would have been for several pints if not gallons.

The Court Rolls do not mention The Coach and Horses by name even though it appears in the 1785 Licensed Victuallers Recognizances. The property belonged between 1780 – 1784 to Mr Richard Stibbing, coachman, when it passed to Mrs Elizabeth Hornsby who held it until 1804. The landlord from 1780 until 1804 was Mr Thomas Kelsey (victualler). The next owner was Mr Francis Hornsby who sold it to Mr John Waring in 1807. The landlord from 1805 until 1811 was Mr Thomas Goff. Other landlords have been 1812 - 1817 Mr Thomas Souster, 1818 – 1824 Mr Philip Butler, 1825 Mrs Elizabeth Butler, 1826 – 1827 Mr James Belsham, 1828 – 1845 Mr John Brown, 1851 Mrs Ann Brown, 1860 Mr William Walter Richards, 1865 – 1872 Mr Joseph Seymour.

From 1873 Young and Bainbridge had a leasehold interest in The Coach and Horses for a period of twenty one years at a rental in the sum of £161 which was to be paid quarterly to Mary Scott Waldo her heirs and assigns. The landlords during this time were, 1873 Mrs Harriet Hayden, June 1876 J Matthews, September 1878 B Mollett, Christmas 1879 Ann Blake, Christmas 1880 Mr Edward Millsum, November 1889 Mr Frank Marfleet, March 1896 Mrs S A Marfleet. In April 1897 Young and Bainbridge paid £6400 to obtain the freehold of the Coach and Horses.

In 1895 the public house served as the headquarters of the Barnes Cycling Club.

The landlords since then have been, June 1897 George Sidney Knight, March 1900 Mrs Sarah Ann Knight, 1902 Mrs Sarah Ann Davis, August 1908 E F Marfleet, 1913 S A Emnett, and 1935 Mr C Everson, after his death in 1946 his widow Frances Magdalene Everson took over. Mr John Everson became joint licensee with his mother in 1950 to run the public house. When John Everson retired as tenant in June 1983 a family link stretching back nearly fifty years was broken.

The next landlord was Mr Tom Moore.

Drinkers in Barnes have gone global, and it has nothing to do with expanding beer bellies. The Coach and Horses has broadcast live over the internet allowing people all over the world to

The Coach and Horses - High Street, Barnes - c 1908-13

The Coach and Horses - High Street, Barnes - c 1960 - Looking east from The Coach and Horses to Lifford Place

watch the goings on at the High Street public house.

Landlady Karen Messit said "As far as we know it's the first public house in the country to go live on the internet. It was my husband Jeff's idea and luckily one of our regulars owns an internet provider and he set the whole thing up. The computer has been set up in one corner of the bar so that patrons can log on to the chat room and chat on line, there are signs outside and inside the public house advising patrons that we go on line between 7 pm and 11 pm. We just show the main area so there will still be corners for privacy. There has been a good reaction from our regulars – they seem to think it's great fun and look forward to communicating with friends and family in other countries. It will be available every week for the first two months of the year 2000 after which time it will be reviewed."

The Coach and Horses 2000

The Halfway House   24 Priest Bridge

Landlord:-   1863 - 1867   Mr Thomas Edward   Owner Joseph Pocock

The Deed of Enfranchisement dated 25 July 1881 between the Earl Spencer, K. G. and Charles Henry Phillips does refer to the fact that the property formerly known as The Jolly Gardeners now known by the sign of The Halfway House, was in the possession of Mr Joseph Porter, (1882) and that Mr C. H. Phillips became tenant on 31 October 1872.

Landlords:-   1890 - 1891   Mrs Anne Porter   Owner Richard Phillips
                1900 - 1921   Mr Samuel Porter

The old public house was very dark and a bit tatty, probably dating back quite a way, the principal customers always seemed to be old men in "flat hats" and chokers and smoking clay pipes!

The present building dates from 1938 and was the last remaining free house in the area, the owner being Mr John Beard who imported his own wines. At The Halfway House the landlord sold port and sherry at 7d per glass, as well as Younger's Scotch Ale and Flowers Bitter, as there was at that time only a beer and wine licence. There were two bars both well patronised.

The Halfway House was managed by Whitbread London Ltd., but the title deeds are held in the name of Whitbread & Co Ltd. The actual conveyance to the Whitbread Group was dated 24 May 1949 from a Mr John Beard of The Foresters Arms, 76 Mitcham Road, Tooting to Whitbread Properties Ltd., at The Brewery, Chiswell Street, EC1 for the sum of £18,000.00 for "all that messuage at Peasebridge otherwise Priestbridge, Mortlake in the county of Surrey, formerly copyhold by the Manor of Wimbledon but now enfranchised and used and occupied as a beer house formerly known as The Jolly Gardeners but now known by the sign of The Halfway House."

The Halfway House, after a four - week closure for a total refurbishment which included repainting, the installation of new furniture and light fittings and repositioning the bar at a cost of more than £60,000, re-opened its doors as a cask and ale house for real ale lovers on Thursday 13 April 1995. The manager of the Whitbread Medway Inns public house, Michael Thompson, said "We are sure that our regular patrons will be pleased with the changes and as we are near the hospital and college we hope to attract a wide cross section of new customers as well".

In June 1998, landlady and landlord Jill and Michael Thompson were pleased to hand over a cheque in the sum of £2.500.00 to Sheila Webb, who accepted it on behalf of The Guide Dogs for the Blind Association. The money had been raised by the customers organising various fund - raising events over the past 128 months, and paid for the training of a two year old retriever called Windsor and settlement with a visually impaired person.

The Halfway House - Priest Bridge - c 1950 Reproduced by kind permission of Whitbread

The Halfway House - Priest Bridge - 1999

The Manor Arms   Railway Side

The earliest reference to The Manor Arms is in the 1881 census.

The Manor Arms is currently owned by Courage but prior to 1943 it may well have been owned by Hodgsons brewery in Kingston.

Landlord:-   1960   L S Jefferies

The regulars at The Manor Arms public house were horrified when they learnt that their local was to be renovated – and the landlord was not to keen on the idea either. But there was no choice in the matter and by August 1982 when it had been completed, everyone was very pleased with the final result.

Mr George Bowles, the licensee, said he was worried when Courage Brewery told him they wanted to knock down the adjoining wall of the cottage to enlarge the bar. The public house is a real local, and its tiny bar, in what used to be the front room of a Victorian cottage, was popular. "I really thought it would ruin the character of the place", said Mr Bowles, "but now that it is finished I really like it, and so do my customers."

The bar is now larger and more comfortable, there are new purpose built toilets and a new cellar. The decoration has ensured the character has not changed and, with Laura Ashley wallpaper and tasteful decorations, the public house is now more similar to a Victorian drawing room than it was before.

The renovation had been going on since November 1981 and in August 1982 was nearly complete, but the public house had not been closed at all. "That is the only thing I would do differently if I had to do it again", said Mr Bowles. "I would close the place down for a few weeks and get it over and done with. This lot has driven me mad."

A keen cook, Mr Bowles was well known for his barbecues. These would continue once the new garden was completed and in addition, there were traditional home-made British meals like shepherd's pie and beef stew at lunchtimes and in the evenings.

John Wimble had his sights on a dream public house, one that he termed the "average local boozer" where pensioners and youngsters alike could enjoy a good pint and wholesome food. Sometime during October 1984 John Wimble bought the lease of the then closed Manor Arms, situated in a quiet pedestrian byway and which at that time still bore signs of its former Victorian glory: the tiled walls and splendid wooden bar.

The regulars at The Manor Arms in January 1985 were pleased to hear that the new landlord John Wimble would carry on running it as a traditional village public house.

The Manor Arms - Railway Side - Barnes - Looking west

Landlord:-   1987 -   Mr Granger

In January 1998, Landlady Lynne Granger praised the regulars for their generous contributions to pub fund raisers. The hampers handed out to local pensioners in time for Christmas 1997 took the ten year total up to three hundred.

The Red Lion   2 Castelnau

Sometime in 1835 a disastrous fire occurred at The Red Lion, then a thatched hostelry known as The Strugglers. Following this the landlord, Mr William Padgett, gave notice at a Vestry Meeting on 3 November of that year that at a future meeting he "will move that an engine be provided for the purpose of extinguishing fires that may accidentally occur in the Parish". However no further mention is recorded on the subject of a fire engine for over thirty years.

Landlords:-   1833 - 39   Mr William Padgett
               1841   Mr William Charingbold
               1845 - 51   Mr Stephen Eastwood   Owner:- Colebrook
               1860   Mr Robert Hammond
               1862   Mr George Edward Sewell
               1864 - 68   Mr Peter Coulston
               1870 - 72   Mrs Caroline Coulston
               1873 - 82   Mr James Bendel

The Red Lion was let and assigned to a number of landlords until the Church Commissioners sold it in 1957 to the Cannon Brewery Company.

Landlord:-   1882 - 84   Mr Henry Whittick

The Red Lion in 1883 had a skittle alley and after the Barnes Tricycle meet on Saturday 26 May of that year several of the clubs had tea there after which the South London Tricycle Club and North London Tricycle Club jointly occupied the skittle alley, and made the best of a damp evening.

Landlords:-   1886   Mrs Martha Griffiths

An advertisement appeared in the Mortlake and Barnes Guardian, a short - lived local paper, on 30 March 1889.
> LEAP FOR LIFE! From a Balloon 5,000 feet above the earth with a PARACHUTE by a World famed Aeronaut, C. W. WILLIAMS, (of the firm of Williams and Young).
> 43 Descents made in Two Seasons.
> Alone worth the price of admission, to see the inflating process, which takes but 30 minutes.
> The ascent will take place from the grounds of The RED LION HOTEL, Bridge Road, Barnes about one hour after the conclusion of the Oxford and Cambridge Boat Race. Admission to the Grounds, 6d. Reserved enclosure, 1s. Balcony of the hotel, 2s. 6d.

In its next issue, the Mortlake and Barnes Guardian, had this to say about the jump: "The Parachute performance, as we anticipated in our last issue, drew crowds to the grounds of

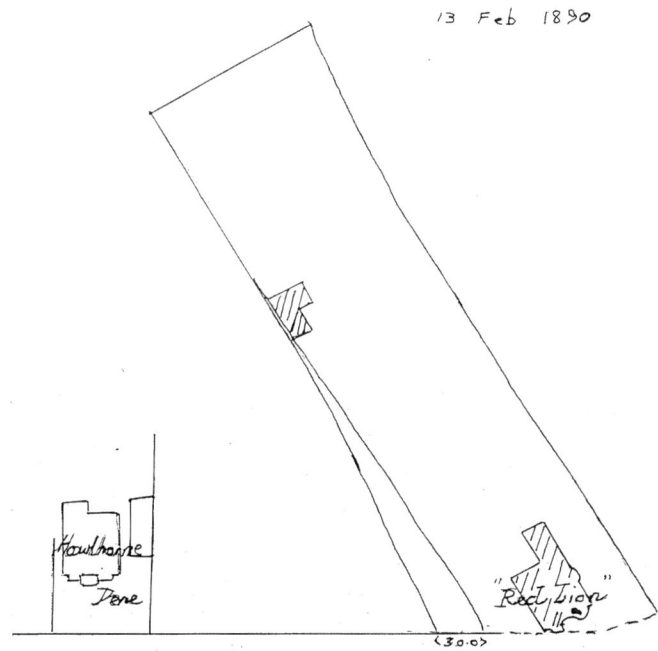

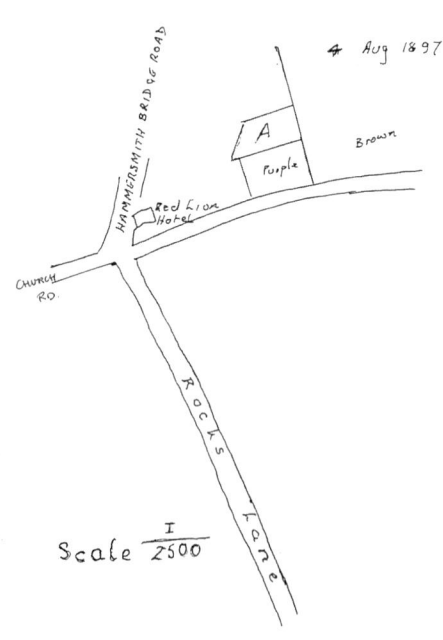

The Red Lion - Barnes - c 1772 - by S H Grimm - Reproduced by kind permission of the British Museum

The Red Lion and entrance to Ranelagh - Barnes - c 1920

The Red Lion on Saturday. The great influx of visitors attending the boat race had, of course, much to do with the results in this respect; but apart from every other consideration, the cleverness of the performance was of itself sufficient to overcrowd the grounds, which, unfortunately, are all too limited for such an exhibition."

Landlord:-   1893   Mary Ann Llewellyn   Owner:- Mr C S Newton

An advertisement appeared in the Richmond Herald on 8 September 1893 stating that the proprietress Mary Ann Llewellyn had made the following improvements to the property. A new billiard room and new saloon bar were available to patrons, whilst outside there was an open air pavilion leading to extensive gardens and shooting gallery. Teas were also supplied.

In 1898 the public house served as the headquarters of the Barnes Cycling Club.

Landlords:-   1921   Mr George E Shearman
                 1939   Mr Sidney V Bailey

The Red Lion is on the right hand side of the west gate of Barn Elms. It has been with The Boileau near the bridge, the temporary hostel of many a sturdy champion of the ring, the running track, and the river. Sayers, Heenan, Brettle, Mace, Goss, Tom King Renforth and others of the earlier pugilists and athletes are said to have put up at these inns, and to have used the local stretch of road between them as their daily training ground.

Mr John Friel, the owner of The Red Lion, Free House, was forced to sell the property after his father, who had bought the pub in 1952, died, and on Saturday 1 July 1978 the public house changed hands after being run as a family business for twenty six years. The new owner was Mr Roger Green, the Chairman of a building contractors, who intended to continue running the public house as a free house in partnership with his sister and brother - in-law.

The Red Lion is now owned by the Chiswick Brewery firm of Fuller Smith & Turner Ltd., who acquired it in 1978.

During the five years from 1982 until Saturday 11 April 1987 that Mr John Blackwell and his wife, Audrey, have been at The Red Lion, the pub had raised enough cash to purchase no fewer than four dogs for the Guide Dogs for the Blind Association at the cost of £1000.00 each. Other charities have also benefited from the pub's constant fund - raising efforts including the nearby Beverley House old people's home which received a new music centre.

Landlord:-   1987   Peter Boutelout

The Rose of Denmark   28 Cross Street

Landlords:-   1939   John Butler
               1960   H P Cooper

The former show jumper and event rider Noel Morton, took over the public house and spent four weeks restoring the premises to its former Victorian splendour. He opened the doors of The Rose of Denmark for the first time as a tenant on Friday 24 September 1982 with wine and beer at half price between 7 pm and 8 pm.

Landlords:-   1986   Mrs Dorothy Arnold
               1988   Mr Patrick Joseph Cunningham

At Richmond on Tuesday 4 April 1989, a North American Mr Stephen Glen Abrahamson with his wife were granted a Protection Order, a temporary licence to sell alcohol.

               1995   P Austin and C Wright

The Rose of Denmark run a football team and in 1986 they were playing in the West Fulham League.

The Rose of Denmark

The Sun Inn   Church Road

Although the Barnes Vestry normally met in the Church, there were four occasions when it moved elsewhere. On 26 December 1753 it "adjourned to the Coffee House" but the meeting was held to be illegal through being held on licensed premises and the decisions had to be taken to the Quarter Sessions to be legalised. However, they again met "at the Coffee House" on 8 February 1756 and on 21 March, of the same year the meeting was held at The White Horse, (where this was has yet to be established). On 21 July 1771 the Barnes Vestry met "at the Coffee House in lieu of the Church." The main reason for holding these meetings outside the Church was that the fabric was under repair and reference to the architects concerned, including Hardwick, Dance and Couse, appear in the minutes.

The Barnes Churchwardens' accounts of 2 October 1776 refer to beer from The Sun, 1s 8d. Unfortunately these accounts do not give any indication of the volume of beer supplied for this sum. No doubt it would have been for several pints if not gallons.

Landlords:-
	1785 - 1804	Mr Samuel Gatwood
	1805 - 1812	Mr William Hitchings
	1813 - 1814	Mr John Stokes
	1815 - 1822	Mr William Goddard
	1823 - 1827	Mr William Royal

In 1829 it came into the possession of John Souster, who presided as landlord from 1829 - 1842 and the name was changed to The Sun Coffee House and premises. In 1832, the name was altered to The Rising Sun public house but in the following year it finally became The Sun Inn.

John Biggs (1757 - 1837) directed that the sum of twenty pounds be expended by his executors for a dinner for the undertaker, (coffin) bearers and persons assisting at his funeral and for all my work people on the day of my funeral for such dinner to be at The Sun Inn, Barnes Green. (Extract from the Will of John Biggs dated 21 March, 1835).

The above statement clearly shows that, just as today, The Sun Inn was serving food as well as drink in the early nineteenth century.

A Deed of Covenant dated 1 December 1802 concerns the surrender of the premises called The Sun Inn Public House or Coffee House occupied then by Samuel Gatwood and a messuage and shop adjoining, then occupied by ....Biss, an under tenant of Gatwood, to the use of John Edward Waring of Barnes, brewer for £840.

The Sun Inn was used as an 'office' by the Tithe Commissioners when they came to Barnes to assess the amount of tithe rent to be paid to the church on the agricultural land in the parish,

The Sun Inn - Church Road - Barnes - c 1960

and as a meeting place for those parishioners who wished to protest against their assessment. From 1831 Young and Bainbridge had a leasehold interest in The Sun Inn, and held it until 1908 when the owner became the Cannon Brewery Company. The landlords during this time were:-

	1860 - 1863	Mr Thomas Hill	
	1865 - 1873	Mr James Culverwell	(Licensed victualler)
20 Nov	1874 - 76	Mr John Claydon	
Dec	1876 - 1877	F Chalk	
27 Sept	1877 - 82	Mr Charles Wagnell	
	1882 - 1888	Mr Christopher Pike	
May	1888 - 1902	Mr Alexander H Jackson	

The Sun Inn was enfranchised by Edwin Richardson Goolden in 1896 and at that time comprised "that messuage or tenement called or known by the sign of The Sun Inn as the same is situated overlooking Barnes Green as is now or late was in the tenure or occupation of A H Jackson, together with the premises in the rear consisting of stabling, coach house, forge, sheds, yard, crown bowling green and garden."

Landlords:-	May 1902 - 1905	Mrs S A Davies	
	January 1906	J Hulbert	
	3 June 1908	K Harding	(Wine and Spirit Merchant)

The Sun Inn in 1908 presented a far more down to earth appearance than today's patrons might believe, for in that year the forge and stables, then at the west end of the hostelry, were in constant use.

Landlords:-	1912	Mr William Fuller
	1913	Mr George Birchmore
	1928	Mrs Edith Maud Leigh

Bowls was reputedly first played on church greens and then inn greens. The crown bowling green, a rarity in the south, at the rear of The Sun Inn, hidden by a brick wall, still forms part of the Sun Inn grounds. In 1922 after the landlady, Mrs Edith Leigh, had waived the £5:0:0 green rent during the First World War, she suddenly announced her intention to convert the crown bowling green into a tennis court. The suddenness of the notice to quit fell like a bombshell on The Barnes Bowling Club, which had been established in 1776. "It seems little short of sacrilege to abolish this historic green which cannot be replaced," the secretary told a local reporter at the time. In a letter to the Herald signed Bias, another member of the bowling club cried; "The loss of the green would be irreparable" and looked back with nostalgia to the "concerts on the green and the annual dinners" which would be sorely missed. The press coverage and local concern made Mrs Leigh change her mind and she was given a relieved vote of thanks at the club's next meeting. The green is still in regular use during the summer months.

The Sun Inn used to belong to the Cannon Brewery Company until they were taken over by Taylor Walker Ltd., who in turn were taken over by Ind Coope Ltd., in 1959.

Landlord:-   1951 - 1982   Mr L P D Fisher

John and Julie Fisher took over the tenancy of The Sun Inn in October 1982, carrying on a family tradition which began in 1951. Inside the Victorian building the atmosphere was warm and cosy, and the patrons were treated to an excellent selection of hot and cold meals (Monday to Saturday) with bar snacks also available. There was a choice of thirty wines from the bottle, and Taylor Walker and Burton ales.

In August 1987 Mr Len Harris, landlord of The Sun Inn, demonstrated to Ind Coope Burton's head brewer, Mr Peter Sutherland, that he not only kept all of his beers in prefect condition, but also had extensive knowledge of the process and care of cask conditioned ales. Looking after draught Burton Ales takes time and attention to detail. They need to be stored in temperatures between 13 - 15 degrees centigrade and must be sampled daily for clarity, aroma and taste and allowed to settle for a minimum of forty eight hours after a delivery has been made and before serving to the patrons.

After three months of careful monitoring Ind Coope decided that Mr Len Harris knew all about storing and serving cask conditioned beers and that every pint drawn and served over the bar was in prefect condition, and consequently Mr Len Harris was awarded membership of the Draught Burton Ale's Guild of Master Cellar men, this prestigious award is only given to top quality stockists of cask conditioned beer.

In January 1988 Taylor Walker, owners of The Sun Inn had to step down from their original proposals, which were to take out all the eighteenth century features of the public house, including the Georgian staircase, after Richmond Council delivered a preservation order on the famous public house on Christmas Eve. As a consequence Taylor Walker revised their plans and retained the Georgian staircase in a £365,000.00 refurbishment. The work was carried out in close co-operation with English Heritage, who advised on authentic eighteenth century details. If the original item was either lost or not in good condition then an antique replica was purchased to replace it. The Sun Inn was closed for three months whilst the refurbishment was carried out and re-opened at the beginning of June 1988.

The Sun Inn - Church Road - Barnes - c 1913-28

The Sun Inn - Church Road - Barnes - c 1913-28 - Viewed across the pond

Ye White Hart Hotel   The Terrace

"Ye White Hart Hotel" was run by the Warner Family until 4 June 1744 when it passed to Martha Bucknall of Barnes until 17 July 1766, when John Trevy, carpenter, of Putney became the proprietor, of "all that messuage and tenement with the appurtenances situate and being in Coles Corner now called and known by the sign of The White Hart." From 17 October 1772, "in the twelfth year of the reign of our sovereign Lord George III, John Trevy for and in the consideration of the yearly rent of £12:12:0 and covenants leased for a period of forty two years to Henry Hunt, brewer of Barnes, his executors, all that brick messuage or tenement, stable yard and outhouses thereto belonging as they are now situated lying in the Parish of Barnes called or known by the sign of The White Hart. Abutting north on the Thames, south on the highway, west on a triangle leading to the Thames, and east on the premises of Henry Cackerill's all which premises are now in the tenure or occupation of the said Henry Hunt."

The Barnes Churchwardens' Accounts of 13 February 1776 refer to beer from The White Hart, 1s 8d. Unfortunately they do not give any indication of the volume supplied for the sum. No doubt it would have been for several pints if not gallons.

In 1804 The White Hart passed to Mr William Trevy, gentleman of Newington in the County of Surrey who on 30 August 1825, bequested it to his wife Elizabeth, and Joseph Norris.

During the period that John and William Trevy were proprietors of the The White Hart there was a continual procession of landlords namely:- 1780 Mr Walker, 1781 Mr Challands, 1782 - 1784 Mr Smith, 1785 - 1788 Mr William Smith, 1789 - 1790 Mr William Crew, 1791 - 1793 Mrs Lucy Crew, 1794 Mr John Cheetcham, 1795 - 1797 Mr John Harrison, 1798 Mr Thomas Wright, 1799 Mr Robert Owen, 1800 Mr Thomas Wakefield, 1801 - 1802 Mr John Cook, 1803 - 1806 Mr William Clark, 1806 Mr William Mapleden, 1807 Mr John Martin, 1808 Mrs Alice Martin. 1809 - 1815 Mr John Nicholls, 1816 - 1824 Mr William Trevy, 1824 - 1830 Mr James Thornton, 1831 Mr William Trevy, 1831 - 1834 Mr John Trevy, 1835 - 1839 Mr Charles Trevy, 1841 Mr William Brook (victualler) - which suggests that the owners had difficulty in obtaining satisfactory tenants.

On 23 July 1812 the inquest concerning the victims of the D'Antraigues murder on Barnes Terrace was held at The White Hart before Mr Charles Jemmett, coroner for the County of Surrey.

In 1843 Elizabeth Trevy and Joseph Norris put The White Hart up for public auction at Garraway Coffee House in the City of London. At the auction, Mr Joseph Toten, of Barnes, was the highest bidder, paying £304:5:6d, as deposit towards the total sum of £1520:0:0d, payable for copyhold and premises. He had previously been butler to Mrs Clowes who lived in a house, on The Terrace, pulled down when the railway bridge was built. In 1843 Mr Joseph Toten was not only the landlord but also the proprietor of "Ye White Hart". On his death on

A. WILL WINCH,

Wine, Spirit, Bottled Beer, and Cigar Merchant,

"WHITE HART" HOTEL,
BARNES.

PRICE LIST.
WINES.

CLARETS.
	Per doz.
Medoc	16/-
St. Emilion	20/-
St. Julien	20/-
Chateau Leoville	39/-
Reale "Italian"	15/-
Bas, Violet	32/-

SHERRY.
	Per doz.
Good pale	21/-
Fine old	24/-
Vino de pasto	42/-
Fine Amontillado	42/-
Very old Brown	48/-

PORTS.
	Per doz.
Good sound Wine	20/-
Old Firm Crust	24/-
Very Choice	39/-
5 years in bottle.	
Very old Crusted	48/-
White Port	48/-
Very elegant.	
Very old, in Nips	15/-

CABINET PORT FROM THE WOOD A SPECIALITY.

PRICE LIST—WINES—*continued.*

BURGUNDY, &c.
	Per doz.
Macon	24/-
Beaune	36/-
Chablis	30/-
Sparkling Moselle	48/-
,, Hock	48/-
Erbock 1884	39/-
Rhenish 1884	39/-
Devonshire Moselle	30/-

CHAMPAGNES.
	Per doz.
Chateau de Conde	60/-
Gauthier et Cie	68/-
Max Sautaine	72/-
Geisler	78/-
Moet and Chandon	84/-
G. H. Mumm	84/-
Perrier Jouet	88/-
Irroy, Carte d'Or	90/-
Pommery and Greno	114/-

SPIRITS.
WHISKIES.
	Per bot.
John Walker's Kilmarnock, red seal	3/6
,, ,, blue seal	4/6
James Buchanan	3/6
Glen Whisky, silver label	3/6
,, ,, gold label	4/6
Haig and Haig	3/6
,, ,, dump bottles	4/3
,, ,, Old Liqueur Magnums	12/6
John Begg, Lochnagar	3/6
Sir Edward Lee's, Scotch	3/6
Glen Dee Whisky	3/6
Toole's Blend	3/6
Lochdhu	3/3
Magna Charta	4/6
Canadian Club	5/-
Jamie's Dukennet	3/6
,, Imperial Liqueur, 12 years old	4/6

PRICE LIST—WHISKIES—*continued.*
	Per bot.
White Heather, "Pure unblended," very-old	4/6
Greer's O.V.H.	3/6
Geo. Roe's St. Patrick	3/6
Fine Old Dublin	3/6
Geo. Roe's Old Dublin, bonded April, 1873	5/-

BRANDIES.
Fine Old	4/-
Courvoisier's Cognac, 8 years old	5/-
,, ,, 20 years old	6/6
Fine Old Brown Liqueur	6/-

GINS and RUMS.
	Per bot.		Per bot.
Fine London Gin	2/3	Fine Demarara	2/3
Strong Old Tom	2/6	Old Jamaica	2/6
Unsweetened	2/3	Old Vatted Jamaica, special value	3/-
Charles Tanqueray's Noted Unsweetened 22 u.p.	2/6		

LIQUEURS.

Benedictine, Curaçoa, Kumel, Maraschino, Chartreuse (Green or Yellow), Cherry Brandy, Damson Gin, Ginger Brandy, &c., &c.

CIGARS, &c.

British specialties from 12/6 to 21/- per box of 100.

HAVANNAH CIGARS.

Partagas, Bocks, Larranaga's, Murias, Henri Clays, Morales, &c.; Mexican and Dutch Cigars, Cigarettes, &c., &c.

AGENT FOR
HIGNETT'S LIVERPOOL TOBACCOS,
FANCY GOODS, &c., &c.

8 September 1851 he bequeathed the copyhold to his three surviving daughters, one of whom had married Christopher Wilcox who had taken over the tenancy in 1851. Joseph Toten died owing heavy mortgage debts which his daughters were unable to settle and as a result the property was surrendered to the Lord of the Manor, who granted the copyhold to C A Young who was liable to pay off the debts and pay the entry fine as a new copyholder. Christopher Wilcox remained as tenant and was succeeded by his son Tom Wilcox, but the copyhold was held by Charles Allen Young who bequeathed it to his wife Elizabeth Young and his son Charles Florence Young.

On the death of Elizabeth Young, Charles Florence Young was admitted under the terms of her will on 3 May 1873. After a full life as a brewer, vat maker and builder he died in 1890. Under the terms of his will, the trustees gave £20,000 to each of his three daughters, the residue of the property to his widow Mary Ann Young who became copyholder of The White Hart and a codicil granted another £20,000 each to his three daughters and wife. Mary Ann Young paid a fine of £275 to succeed to the copyhold which meant that she, her heirs etc. "were beholden to the Lords by copy of Court Roll all the will of the Lords according to the custom of the said manor by fealty suit of Court the yearly rent of 4d and other customs and services due."

When the Order in Council of 16 January 1873 gave the Ecclesiastical Commissioners authority to "sell or dispose and convey all or part of the said property (which had passed to them from the estates of the Dean and Chapter of St Paul's) to the use of any person or persons desirous or willing to purchase the same," Mrs Mary Ann Young by a deed of enfranchisement dated 21 July 1898 purchased the Lord of the Manor's interest in The White Hart for "the sum of £1,600 to be paid .... to the Bank of England to the Ecclesiastical Commissioners." The Youngs had succeeded in buying "all that messuage or tenement with appurtenances .... lying and being in Coles Corner within this manor commonly called or known by the name or sign of The White Hart" and they held it "as freehold freed and discharged from all fines, quit rents etc." and "all other incidents whatsoever of copyhold or customary tenure."

Landlords:-   1880 – 1884 Mr Richard Crowdy Monk, 1890 Mr Alfred William Winch (he wrote an amusing booklet entitled "Bits about Barnes"), 1897 Mr George Bubear, a champion sculler. Bubear was succeeded by Mr Alfred Horace Brewer in 1902.

The White Hart provided for visitors who came by river rather than traders who tended to go to the Bulls Head. So popular was the former that we read in the West London Sketch of 1 July 1889 that the promised steamboat pier beside The White Hart is still in the process of construction "which will be a great convenience to the inhabitants of Barnes and Mortlake as well as visitors when finished." In the nineteenth century, visitors stood on the Venetian style verandah looking at the pleasure boats on the river or sat inside in the comforting environment of the old Victorian mahogany bar which has since been removed. Today, after a stroll along Barnes Terrace, which itself boasts many eighteenth century houses of different styles, The White Hart is still as welcoming.

ALFRED HAYS' THEATRE PLAN BOOK

'PHONE (CORNHILL) AVENUE 3300
'PHONE (BOND ST.) REGENT 3400

BOAT RACE
(WHITE HART HOTEL, BARNES)

TOWPATH

If you would travel by Rail, Sea, Road or Air, do so through

THOS. COOK & SON LTD.
BERKELEY STREET, PICCADILLY, W.1
Or any Branch

The White Hart - Coles Corner - Barnes - c 1770 - by S H Grimm. - At a spot near the junction of White Hart Lane and The Terrace. The Inn with its royal head is the old Kings Head now rebuilt and named Ye White Hart. - Reproduced by kind permission of the British Museum

The White Hart - River Thames - Barnes - c 1770 - by S H Grimm. - At the boundary junction of Barnes and Mortlake. The four storey building is the old Kings Head now rebuilt and named Ye White Hart. - Reproduced by kind permission of the British Museum

Ye White Hart Hotel - Barnes - At the junction of White Hart Lane and The Terrace.

Ye White Hart Hotel - Barnes - c 1904 - Viewed from across the river from the Chiswick bank. Photograph by Field, Putney

The White Hart, gives the impression of being a more tranquil house, welcoming visitors to Barnes who have come to enjoy the leisure pursuits of the river. The original house, a solid square white building with slate roof and portico to the door which had stood since 1662, was pulled down in 1899 when the present building was constructed. This enormous chateau - sized structure used to be a hotel and thus the present tenants, the Lockwoods, have a generous sized flat. There are one hundred stairs in all and part way up them is a large ballroom, where people used to gather on Wednesdays for old time dancing. At one time the pianist Russ Conway used it as a recording studio and it is still rather difficult to find maximum use for the space.

In the late 19th and early 20th century the most dramatic day of the year was of course the occasion of the Oxford and Cambridge boat race, when supporters crowded the bar after running along the towpath shouting encouragement to the oarsmen. Unfortunately, whether the supporters and their ladies could always succeed in obtaining beer to sup on the verandah or the vantage point of the roof, depended upon the time of the race which in turn depended on the tides. If the race had a late start, the hospitable doors would be closed because the magistrates had refused to allow an extension of hours despite numerous applications. The enthusiasts were then condemned to tea drinking, which William Cobbett viewed "as a destroyer of health, an enfeebler of the frame, an engender of effeminacy and laziness, a debaucher of youth and a maker of misery for old age." But if they were not spared this fate by the tides, it was a great consolation to know that at 5.30 pm hostelries in Barnes and elsewhere on the Thames waited eagerly to welcome and entertain them.

Landlords:-
- November 1930 Mr Edward William Bunten
- February 1943 Mr Arthur Endersby
- January 1948 Mr Frederick Earnest Endersby (Son)
- March 1950 Mr Percival John Greene
- December 1956 Mr Joseph Henry Craston
- April 1960 Mr Eric Hunter Naylor
- February 1963 Mr Deny Edward Morrison
- June 1965 Mr John Henry Lockwood

The White Hart has long been renowned for its beer, but wine lovers would never have made a bee line for the riverside public house. However in June 1998 the manager Stewart Sell picked up the Chairman's Trophy for Wine Excellence after transforming the public house's wine reputation. Stewart Sell was responsible for serving sixteen wines by the glass or bottle, and ran wine tasting courses every other month.

Ye White Hart Hotel - Barnes - c 1960 - The junction of White Hart Lane and The Terrace.

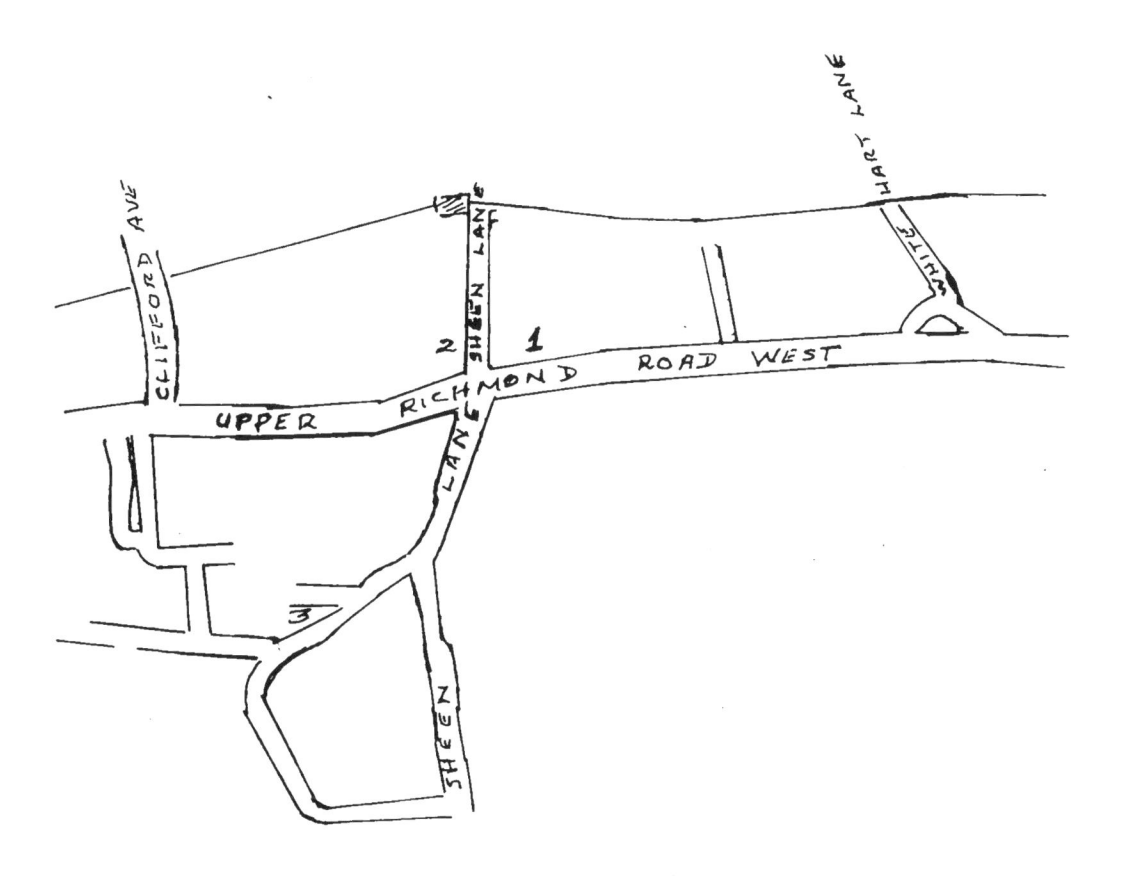

Map of East Sheen showing the location of the present public houses

1 Hare and Hounds   2 Pig and Whistle
3 Plough

East Sheen S W 14

The Hare and Hounds   216 Upper Richmond Road West

The original date of the inn is unknown but it was The Hare and Hounds in 1776. When Palewell Lodge was sold in 1798, the sale particulars stated "a pack of harriers is kept in the neighbourhood" and this could account for the name of the inn.

From 1772 - 1795 a Mr Thomas Bosley occupied the premises as landlord, whether he was the owner is uncertain. From 26 June 1794 and upwards of five weeks not less than eight men and seven horses belonging to the Eleventh Regiment of the Light Dragoons were quartered and billeted at The Hare and Hounds, which at that time had eight regular standings. By 1799 the property was in the ownership of Mr John Waring. His tenant at that time was Mr Samuel Ceate who remained in occupation until 1809. Mr John Waring passed the property onto his widow, Mary Waring, who held it from 1810.

Landlords from 1810, Mr Robert Roberts, 1811 - 1815, Mr Thomas Powell, 1815 - 1820, Mr Christopher Cowney who was succeeded by his widow Mrs Mary Cowney. From 1821 - 1828 Mr John Allam was the landlord, living afterwards at the Old Chapel House. Mr John Allam built a small house with a yard on the east side of the hotel where it joined the Church Path. This house and yard were used for some years by Mr Ralph Woodiss as a stonemason's yard. In 1829 Mr John Blanchard became the landlord and remained in occupation until July 1843, for in that year on 20 July Mr John Hammond is recorded as being the landlord. He was succeeded in 1846 by Mr John Gratton who remained until 1862.

When Mr Joseph Medworth, surveyor to the Mortlake District Highway Board, left the board he took a public house in Oxford Street and afterwards one in Compton Street, London. Eventually in 1862 he moved to The Hare and Hounds and was landlord for about five years. In 1867 Mr Joseph Bishop took over as landlord, and during the following year he was succeeded by Mr James Holyard, who remained in occupation until 1890.

The rate books of 25 November 1836, 21 April 1840, 31 May 1855 and 15 May 1863 all state that the owners of The Hare and Hounds are Young and Bainbridge. The rate book of 10 June 1891 states that the owners of The Hare and Hounds are Young & Co.

Lease dated 25 March 1873 states that:

All that messuage, tenement or public house with appurtenances thereto belonging situate and being at East Sheen in the said County of Surrey called or known by the name or sign of The Hare and Hounds as the same were in the tenure or occupation of the widow of Christopher Cowney and now are of Gratton together with all house, outhouses, yards, garden ways and passages.

From the records held at Young & Co's Brewery at Wandsworth we know the names of the landlords at The Hare and Hounds until 1986.

1	December	1892	Mr Arthur S. Perrin
	October	1902	Mr G. F. Coe
	April	1908	Mr F. H. Coe
28	May	1909	Mr J. W. Koklhausen
27	January	1916	Mr E. G. B. Warwick
27	December	1922	Mr H. B. Brodie
17	December	1923	Mrs Katherine Jane Otley
25	August	1927	Mr Charles Newman
16	April	1930	Mr William G. Simmonds
26	March	1968	Mr Dennis Victor Turner

The landlord Mr Arthur S. Perrin, some time between December 1892 and October 1902, was advertising billiards, a bowling green, ping pong tables, a dining saloon, polo stables and other good stabling.

The landlord Mr William Simmonds and his wife were charming people, and during the Second World War it was almost a club as most of the patrons were locals and regular visitors to the public house. They also had an off - licence next door, which the patrons always thought to be the answer to the following:-
During the war, at six pm, opening time, William Simmonds would put up a bottle of whisky and a bottle of gin. The resulting scramble, which was repeated at 9.00pm, was quite something! The bitter drinkers knew to keep clear!

In the garden there was a crown bowling green - a rarity in the south of the country. Also two good billiard tables while it is believed to be the first public house to put a television in the lounge.

When Mr Dennis Turner reached his fourteenth birthday in April 1936, his publican father allowed him to pull his first pint behind the bar of The Plough and Harrow in Battersea Park Road. Fifty years of pulling pints for Dennis has been interrupted only by his Second World War service in the Middle East with the Royal Air Force. His memories include the time when his brother, Victor, was buried alive in the rubble of The Plough and Harrow when it was demolished by a Luftwaffe bomb. He was dug out by the ARP.

During his time as landlord of The Hare and Hounds, Mr Dennis Turner, was chairman of the Richmond and District Licensed Victuallers Association and president of the Ladies Auxiliary, and for six years he was president of the Richmond Friends of Cancer Research.

On Friday 18 December 1981, carol singing from a Young & Co's horse drawn dray was a feature in Mortlake and East Sheen. It was the idea of the brewery and Mr Dennis Turner, licensee, who had organised fund raising events in support of the Imperial Cancer Research

The Hare and Hounds - Upper Richmond Road - East Sheen - was so named in 1776

Fund. The dray left The Hare and Hounds and made its way along Sheen Lane to The Charlie Butler in Mortlake High Street, with a group of charming ladies singing carols.

On 11 April 1986 Mr Dennis Turner celebrated his sixty fourth birthday by working the pumps at The Hare and Hounds where he had been licensee for the past eighteen years. Throughout the licensing hours, Mr Dennis Turner served Young's traditional beers at fifty pence a pint – just above half price – then announced that he was to retire in November.

The Hare and Hounds - Upper Richmond Road West - East Sheen - c 1960

The Pig and Whistle   86 Sheen Lane

Few people raised their glasses to the new Pig and Whistle public house when it opened its doors on 29 September 1988 on part of the former site of The Bull (see past pubs in East Sheen.)

Controversy blew up over the name of this public house when angry Sheen and Mortlake residents claimed that a historical landmark and link with the past had been lost. "There is a lot of local disappointment over the choice of The Pig and Whistle as a name, which people are saying is contrived and a bit of a frolic. Everyone expected the new public house to be called The Bull," said Mr. Charles Hailstone, a writer and local historian. The manager of The Pig and Whistle, a free house owned by the company Grand Metropolitan, Mr. Bill Muir said: "We have had a lot of curiosity about our name. It was a deliberate policy not to rename the public house The Bull. We wanted a light hearted name and a chance to change the clientele that The Bull used to attract." Defending the company's choice of name still further, Area Manager Mr. Richard Edwards, said "The Pig and Whistle is one of the oldest public house names around and we chose it because it is so traditional. We intended the name to be amusing, after all we are in business to entertain."

The Pig and Whistle in 1999 was owned by Scottish and Newcastle Retail.

The Plough   42 Christ Church Road

The Plough Inn is situated on the corner of Christ Church Road and Well Lane and its front faces southwards. It appears to consist of what was once three Queen Anne cottages, and is one of East Sheen's oldest inns.

In 1846 when Mr Jepe Nalder Bell was the landlord this public house was known by the sign of The Plough and Harrow.

From 31 May 1855 to 1867 Mr John Sharp was the owner as well as the landlord.

Landlords:-		1872	Mrs Louisa Sharp
		1882	Mr John Clifford
	30 June	1884	Mr William Smith
	9 September	1886	Mr Frederick Stone
		1890	Mr John Sim
		1891	Mr Arthur Isaac

The rate book of 10 June 1891 states that Bessie Rudkin is the owner of The Plough.

| Landlords:- | 1900 | Mr John Hall |
| | 1902 - 1903 | Mr Charles Higham |

Mr Thomas Dixon moved from The Wheatsheaf in Sheen Lane to The Plough in 1920 and was there until 1939.

The Plough Inn was, in the 1930's and 1940's, another "club" type public house. In the late 1940's when the landlady was Mrs Dixon, she was always known to the regulars as "Auntie". The house was really run by Eva, the barmaid, a lady of great character and somewhat generous proportions. She knew all the patrons by name many of whom used to keep their own tankard there. She knew which was which and what to put in which tankard.

Sometime around 1946 there was a serious shortage of beer, so Eva would draw a pint or two and put them aside for later! Most of the patrons were locals, there being no petrol and few cars. Sometimes the variety actress Billie Houston, who lived in Fife Road, would set the place going, and occasionally her sister Rene would visit and the two together were great entertainment.

After the Second World War, by 1947 - 1948, the scene changed, Eva retired. The two bars were later made into one, though it was noticeable that the old "public" patrons still used the end of the bar where the public bar had been situated. The landlord in 1960 was Mr H M Johnson.

Mr Harold Perkins with his wife Peggy moved from The Lass of Richmond Hill in 1964 to take over the running of The Plough where this popular licensee died on 2 July 1966 at the age of 59.

Licensee Mrs Peggy Jones (1966 – 1970) said goodbye to her regulars at The Plough, many of whom, were sorry to see her go, and retired from the business which had been her life for the past thirty three years.

The new faces behind the bar belonged to Mr Frank Westby and his wife Philomena. They were already well known in East Sheen because they had been running the nearby Derby Arms (see East Sheen past pubs) for the past four and a half years.

In September 1990 a planning application was submitted by the new landlord Brian O'Donovan to build a new single storey bottle store on top of which would be sited a small hotel extension comprising four single bedrooms for an overnight stay by staff and members of the public. He now has a new feather to add to his cap – that of owning one of the oldest buildings in East Sheen. For, just by chance, while building work was being carried out at The Plough, a timber strut dating back to around 1530 was discovered. The sixteenth century timber, which forms the entire middle strut of the popular East Sheen hostelry, had been covered up behind a bathroom wall. Now, it is on show for all the guests staying at the public house to enjoy. English Heritage were called in to inspect the beam, and supplied Mr O'Donovan with a recipe for wattle and daub to replace the material damaged during refurbishment work in 1840.

Mr Paul Calvocoressi of English Heritage could not put an exact date on the beam but he believed it was possibly sixteenth century although it could be earlier or later. "This type of construction that occurred then has quite a date range. Certainly it is interesting and seems to be in good hands," said Mr Calvocoressi. He added that the beam was fairly unusual in Greater London. "I would not have expected it to turn up in The Plough at all and this is quite exciting."

"It is very much a feature for those staying here to see the beam," said Mr O'Donovan who added; "I do not know of a house in our particular area that is as old as this."

Bar staff at The Plough were looking back during the week 8 – 15 September 1995, when they found two crumbling yellow newspapers dating back almost fifty years, hidden beneath their shelves. Catering manager Miss Miranda Mills explained "We were just cleaning behind the shelves which had been ripped out when we found a copy of The Daily Herald from 1949 and an Evening News from 1952. Its quite interesting – there was one story about a woman who got fined £5 by the RSPCA for tying her dog up with a rope and another about new London Buses which were going to replace Trams." Miss Mills decided that she would hide a copy of the Richmond and Twickenham Times behind the new shelves.

The Plough and Merton Cottages - Christ Church Road - East Sheen - c 1902-03

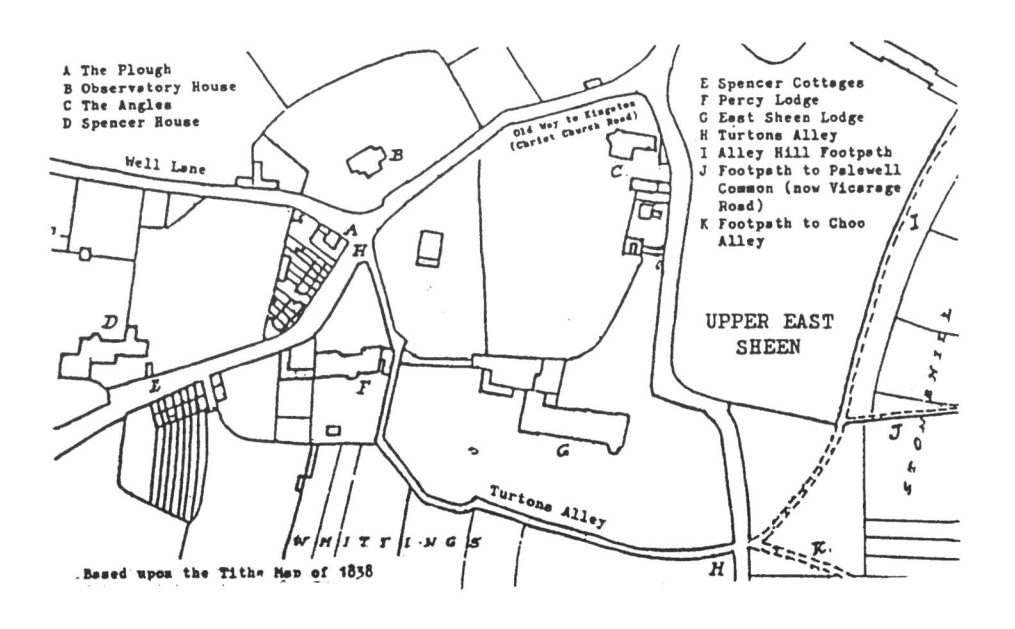

A The Plough
B Observatory House
C The Angles
D Spencer House

E Spencer Cottages
F Percy Lodge
G East Sheen Lodge
H Turtons Alley
I Alley Hill Footpath
J Footpath to Palewell Common (now Vicarage Road)
K Footpath to Choo Alley

UPPER EAST SHEEN

Based upon the Tithe Map of 1838

The Plough and Merton Cottages - Christ Church Road - East Sheen - c 1916

The Plough and Merton Cottages - Christ Church Road - East Sheen

The Plough - Christ Church Road - East Sheen - c 1960

The Plough - Christ Church Road - East Sheen - c 1968

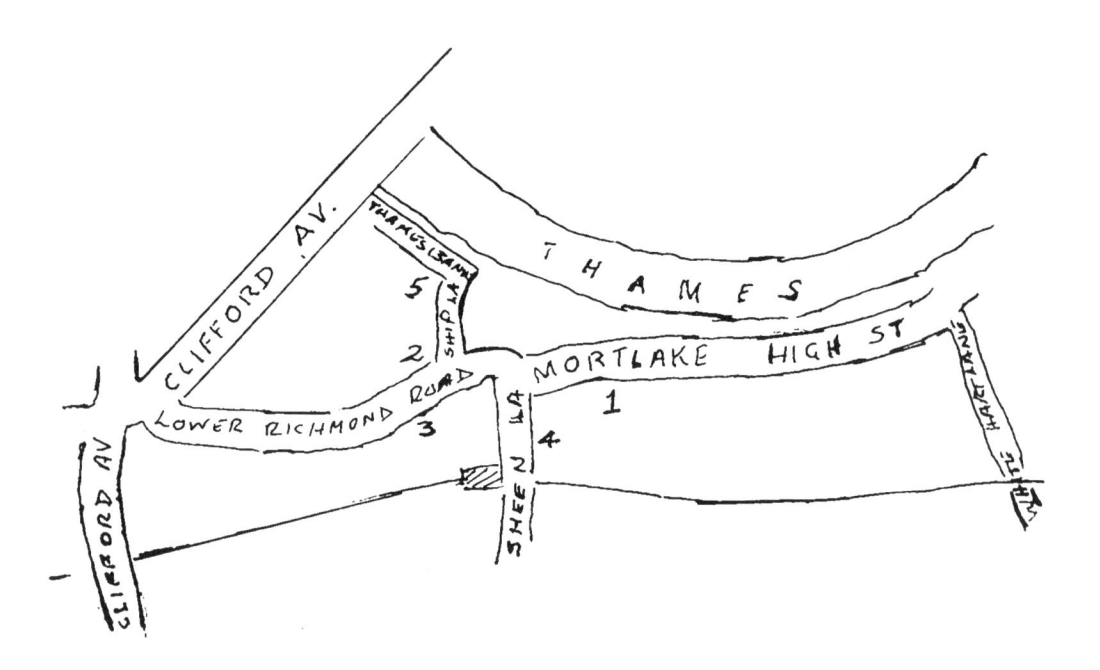

Map of Mortlake showing the location of the present public houses

1 Charlie Butler   2 Jolly Gardeners   3 Jolly Milkman
4 Railway Tavern   5 Ship Hotel

Mortlake S W 14

The Charlie Butler   40 Mortlake High Street

The Charlie Butler replaced The Old George (see past pubs in Mortlake) as part of an agreement between the Council and Young & Co's Brewery when the road was widened and The Old George had to be demolished. The doors were first opened to the public from midday 2 August 1968 under the tenancy of Thompson and Dempsey Limited. The public house derives its name from the Head Horse Keeper, Charlie Butler, who worked for forty three years at Young & Co's Brewery in Wandsworth. It was under his direction that the horses won more show prizes than any other brewery team before or since.

Irish born Edward Dempsey, the first licensee, had been at The Charlie Butler for over sixteen years, when he retired at the weekend 23/4 February 1985. Ned who saw active service with the Beach Group in the World War Two invasion of Normandy, once achieved a lifelong ambition by singing on the stage of The Royal Opera House, Covent Garden, at an informal party held by his friends among the cast. His rendering, in keeping with his lively sense of humour, was "Paddy Mcginty's Goat."

Young & Co's Brewery, in February 1985, turned to management with Ian Turner and his wife Mary at the helm, although Edward Dempsey had been asked to retain his presidency of the Mortlake Football Club which is based at the public house.

From 1986 – 88 the landlady was Mrs. Wendy Perkins.

At Richmond Court on Tuesday 27 September 1989, a Protection Order, was granted in favour of Development Manager, Mr. Stephen Gallagher, for a limited period to serve liquor. Mr. Gallagher agreed that the Protection Order was a holding arrangement because the lady of the house had new ideas. The applicant said he had management experience with The Crown at Chertsey and The Green Man at Putney.

The Charlie Butler - Mortlake High Street - c 1969

The Jolly Gardeners   36 Lower Richmond Road

The Jolly Gardeners, situated at the corner of the Lower Richmond Road and Ship Lane, is one of the oldest established public houses of Mortlake. Although the present building with its Tudor style chimneys gives the impression of being a much older property, it in fact dates only from 1922. There has been a public house with the same name on or near the present site since 1794 and before that it was known by the sign of The Three Tuns (see past pubs in Mortlake.)

From 26 June 1794 and for upwards of five weeks not less than seven men and six horses belonging to the Eleventh Regiment of Light Dragoons were quartered and billeted at The Jolly Gardeners, which at that time had no stabling for the horses.

It was sometime during the year 1798 that Mr Richard Bagley, a market gardener of Fulham, who also worked in Barnes at Bagley's Stile and field, together with Mr John Prior, who had maltings in Mortlake and a brewery between Thames Street and Mortlake Street (High Street,) were admitted to The Jolly Gardeners under the conditional surrender of Mr William Richmond, who had malt houses in Mortlake and Barnes together with property in Barnes (Richmond Cottage, Triangle Square, Westfields.)

In September 1802 one Stephen Stilwell murdered his wife there, and consequently was hanged for the offence.

Mr William Burlton was the licensee for only two years (1813 - 1815) before moving to The Rose and Crown at Isleworth, and at that time the owner was Mr George Tritton. Between 1815 - 1822 Mr John Dairy was the landlord, then from 1823 to 16 October 1826 the landlord was Mr William Brady. He was followed by Mr James Grimshaw, it was whilst he was the landlord that on one occasion, through the rising of the Thames, the floor of the bar burst upwards owing to the pressure of air and water.

Young and Bainbridge first leased The Jolly Gardeners in 1833 and their landlord from 1839 - 1840 was Mr William Preble, who was succeeded in 1841 by Mr J Parsons until 1843 when his widow Mrs Emma Parsons took over. She was succeeded by Mr Harding on 21 October 1846.

When Young's Brewery obtained the freehold of The Jolly Gardeners the building that stood there previously was described on 1 July 1857 "as being a snug roadside house which has been rebuilt by us."

Landlords:-   31   May   1855   Mary Field
               7   August   1857   Frances Field
                             1860 – 1865   Misses Fanny & Eliza Field

The first Odd Fellows Lodge set up in Mortlake was The Loyal Penrhyn Lodge on 3 November 1865, which met at The Kings Arms (see past pubs in Mortlake.) The second was the Loyal Pride of Mortlake Lodge, London Unity on 31 July 1867, and they held their meetings at The Jolly Gardeners. The Odd Fellows Lodges were fraternal, benevolent and sickness insurance friendly societies first founded in the 18th century, but later banned. Revived early in the 19th century they were basically men's social clubs – as well as following their original premise to give mutual help in times of death, sickness and unemployment.

Landlords:-				
			1867	Mr James Field
	19	June	1872 - 1891	Mrs Mary Ann Boggia
		June	1895	Mr J William Howard
		November	1899	Mr William John Parker
		March	1920	S Baker
		August	1921	L G Lashman
		May	1922	T P Pearce
		July	1924	W L Swinyard
		March		A J Bristowe
		February	1936	A J Higgs
		February	1939	Mr James William Groome
		May	1939	Mr Thomas Frederick Ingram
		July	1950	Mr James Smith
		March	1966	Mr Henry John Carpenter
		October	1968	Mr Frederick C Robert Holloway
		May	1982	Jean and Keith Richards

During June 1982 voices were raised in song when the music started at 8.30pm on Saturday nights. The public house had a piano player, drummer and singer/compere leading community singing of the golden oldies of yesterday. By September the musical entertainment had increased to a Sunday night at 8.30pm when a resident pianist provided the music.

In 1987, during a major renovation and refurbishment of the public house, the screen separating the public and saloon bars was removed.

Landlord:-	June	1993	Mr Michael Barry

The Jolly Gardeners - Littleworth End - Ship Lane looking south with The Jolly Gardeners on the right - From a drawing by Albert Betts

The Jolly Gardeners - Mortlake - Stood at the corner of Lower Richmond Road and Ship Lane - c 1899-1919 - Rebuilt in 1922

The Jolly Gardeners - Lower Richmond Road - Mortlake - c 1969

The Jolly Milkman   1 Lower Richmond Road

Landlord:-   1871 - 1872   John Denby

Mr John Firmston, who had previously been the last landlord at The Kings Arms (1855 - 67) and landlord at The Queens Head, settled down in the small beer house at the west end on the south side of Lower Richmond Road called The Jolly Milkman in 1878, where he died on 31 May 1888, in his seventy seventh year. His widow took over the tenancy.

Landlords:-	1891	Mr Edward Day
	1895	Mr Charles Amos
	1900	Mr William Amos
	1902 - 1903	Mr Edward Kisby
11 September	1907 - 1917	Mr Richard Davis Foster
		Mrs Eliza Foster
	1924	Mr Frederick Longman
	1931	Mr Richard Davis Foster
	1932	Mr John James Wood
	1939	Mr William Crane
	1960	K L Balls
October	1980 - 1982	Mr Graham Marriner

Attractive Margaret Marriner, full-time barmaid, and wife of licensee Mr Graham Marriner was the winner of the 1982 Babycham Barmaid of the Year Competition. The judges had a tough job separating the four finalists. Only the business sense/bar know-how section gave Margaret the victory as her twelve years experience in the trade showed.

This public house was for many years owned by Watney's and in the late 80's or early 90's became part of Grand Metropolitan, who in turn sold their interest in this public house to Scottish and Newcastle.

The Magic Pub Company, having acquired this public house from Scottish and Newcastle, changed the sign and name to The Pickled Newt on Tuesday 5 September 1995. Their landlord from February 1995 was Mr Paul Sharpe. This name change coincided with a complete refurbishment including a new menu and the addition of pictures on the walls and objects relating to fishing on the ceiling. The beer tasted the same, but for the regulars of The Jolly Milkman - the only public house in England to bear that name - things turned sour. They were dismayed to find that the familiar Jolly Milkman sign with the friendly milkman had been replaced with one declaring it to be The Pickled Newt, with a predictable picture of a newt. A campaign of protest letters from perturbed regulars to the management ensued, they even raised a petition calling for the removal of the much loathed name, but the company would not budge on its decision.

Mr Melvin Waite arrived in November 1995 as the new landlord and walked right into the middle of the argument over the name. It was due to the extensive efforts of Mr Waite, who wrote a confidential internal report and one of his regulars, Jo Billingham, who wrote a letter to the Managing Director, so that they would both land on the Managing Director's desk on the same day. The result was that the Company finally changed their minds and agreed to reinstate the old name. On 1 May 1996 this house reverted back to its original name, with a buffet and live music in the evening to celebrate.

The ownership of The Jolly Milkman was transferred from the Magic Pub Company on 18 June 1996 to Greene King Plc.

The Jolly Milkman - Lower Richmond Road - Mortlake - Milk cart visible though gateway -
By kind permission of Courage

The Jolly Milkman - Lower Richmond Road - Mortlake - 1969

The Jolly Milkman - Lower Richmond Road - Mortlake - 1998 - Interior

The Railway Tavern   11 Sheen Lane

Formerly a private dwelling built c 1800, after the railway came in 1846, the place was opened as The Railway Tavern beer house by a man named Wheatley. He was a great handbell ringer. Some little time afterwards he was accidentally drowned in the river near The Queens Head.

1872	Mr John Albert Coles
1896	Mr George Turner Wheatley
1900 – 03	Mr Ernest Cole

The Railway Tavern was owned by The Royal Brewery (Brentford) Ltd. and their landlords were Mr L C G Hopperton, 1931 Mr Edwin James Carman, and 1935 Mr Frederick Shadrack Collins.

1960   Mrs J F Collins

The Land Registry document shows Mr Cooper purchased the property from Courage Barclay & Simonds Limited but does not give a definitive date. On 10 December 1984 T G Cooper formerly trading as T G Cooper Leisure & Company sold The Railway Tavern to Hall & Woodhouse Limited who are the current owners.

Landlords:-   1999   C C Green and N L Williams

The Railway Tavern - Sheen Lane

The Ship Hotel   10 Thames Bank

Taking a diagonal route across Mortlake Green from the railway station, you will come out in Lower Richmond Road, opposite the entrance to Ship Lane. Walk down this lane towards the river bank, and at its end almost directly opposite the finish of the boat race course, is The Ship Hotel.

In 1781 the landlord of The Ship was Mr Thomas Hill.

From 26 June 1794 and for upwards of five weeks not less than eight men and eight horses belonging to the Eleventh Regiment of Light Dragoons were quartered and billeted at The Ship, which at that time had six regular standings.

The property was owned in 1812 by Halford and Weatherstone; whilst the landlord then was Mr John Smith, and from 1813 - 1814 the landlord was Mr Isaac Hall. In 1814 Mr Richard Pike took over as the landlord. The property passed in 1815 to the ownership of Messrs Halford & Co., and Mr Richard Pike continued as their landlord until 1820.

The Benevolent Brothers Friendly Society was set up in Mortlake in 1816 and held their meetings at The Ship Inn. This Society was basically a men's social club which existed to give mutual help in times of death, sickness and unemployment and was supported by people above the actual poverty line.

In 1821 Mr John Hammond took over as the landlord and in the following year the public house is clearly recorded by the name of The Ship. Sometime during 1826 Mr John Hammond left The Ship to become the landlord at The Bull, for in that year Mr James Rogers is recorded as his replacement. Between 1829 - 1841 Mr Charles Parker was the landlord. The rate book of 25 November 1836 states that the owners of The Ship are Messrs Halford and Topham. On 30 April 1842 Mr Samuel Larkin took over and remained there until 1845 - 1846 when Mr J Arnell succeeded him.

The landlord in 1851 was Mr Robert Grombs. The rate book dated 31 May 1855 states that the property is owned by Messrs Phillips and Wigan, however no landlord is recorded at this time.

On 12 June 1855 Mr Alexander Thomas Blake became the landlord, probably the first to occupy the present building. On 7 August 1857 Mr Thomas Twogood became the landlord and he was followed by Mr George Twogood in 1860. In 1862 Mr George Howell took over to be replaced in 1865 by Mr William Gray, who remained until 1867.

Landlords:-   1871   Mr Samuel Phillips
               1872   Miss Alice Martiell

The Ship Inn - Thames Bank - Mortlake - 1825 - From a wash drawing by James Bourne

The Ship Inn - Thames Bank - Mortlake - Reproduced by kind permission of Courage

1876	Mr George Sharp
1882 - 1883	Mr Edwin Lucus
1884	Mr Richard Hill
1890 - 1891	Mr Albert Thomas Chesefield
1895	Mr Joseph H Kinsley

Ownership of The Ship Hotel passed in 1890 - 1891 to Watney & Co., when the Phillips and Wigan Brewery business was incorporated.

Landlords:-	1900	Mr Frank Whitehead
	1902	Mr William Brown
	1903	Mr Charles Edward Ward

Even in the twentieth century licensees occasionally got into trouble with the law. At an adjourned licensing session in March 1937 an application was made on behalf of the licensee Mrs Olivette Rose Foster for the renewal of the licence, and to tend her sincere regret at having given occasion to receive a caution from the police authorities. The facts out of which the caution arose occurred on Christmas Eve, when Mrs Foster kept open after normal closing time of 10.30 pm. The police visited the premises about 10.45 pm and found very little trade with only about half a dozen people in the house. Although Mrs Foster had been in the licensing trade for nearly forty years she had never previously kept open on Christmas Eve; she was under the impression that it was an automatic extension and that there was no need for a formal application to be made to the Commissioner of Police.

The Ship was for many years owned by Watney's and in the late 1980's or early 1990's became part of Grand Metropolitan, who in turn sold their interest in this public house to Scottish and Newcastle.

The Ship Inn - Thames Bank - Mortlake - With Cromwell House beyond - From a painting by Edward Matthews - 1890

Past Pubs

Map of Barnes showing the location of the past public houses

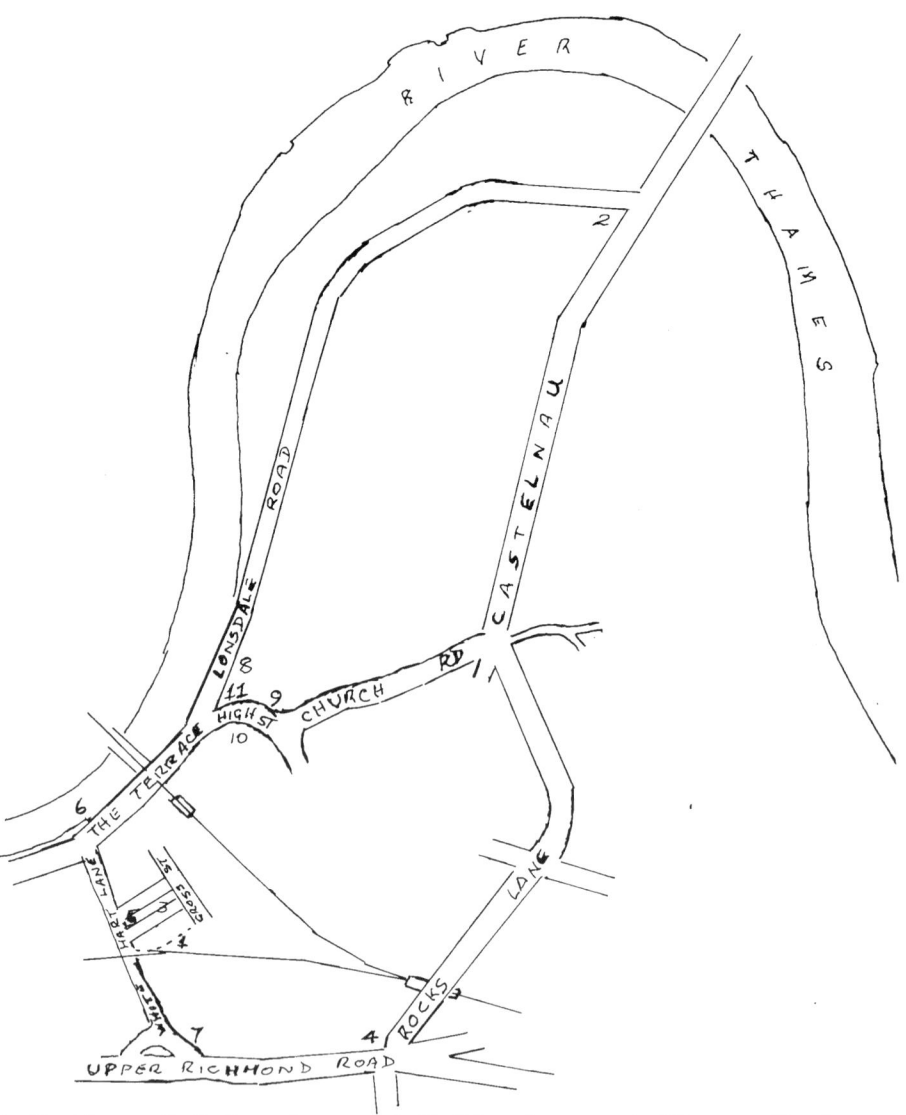

1 Beehive   2 Boileau Arms   3 Builders Arms   4 Clipstons Beerhouse
5 Edinburgh Castle   6 Kings Arms   7 Market Gardener
8 Rayne Deer   9 Rose   10 Three Cups Tavern   11 Watermans Arms

Barnes SW 13

The Beehive   36 Railway Side

The Beehive no longer exists as a public house, although the building it occupied at 5 Holts Cottages still stands today, as a privately owned cottage and retains the name The Beehive above the door.

The Beehive appears to have been no more than a small beerhouse which started up in the latter half of the nineteenth century in a two storey brick terrace cottage with two bay windows on the ground floor, and with sash windows upstairs. Virginia creeper overhung the porch to shelter the drinkers from sun and rain as they sat on an outside bench. It closed its door to the public on 14 December 1970.

Landlords:-
- 1882 - 1891   Mrs Phyllis Webb (Licensed victualler)
- 1900 - 1904   Mr Alfred Potter
- 1905 - 1906   Mr William Bosher
- 1924   Mr George Richard Ruffell (Beer retailer)
- 1932   Mr E J Hill (Beer retailer)
- 1939   Mr Reginald Holt
- 1960   Mrs I K Davy

The former Beehive Inn - Railway Side - Barnes - The day after closure - 1970

The Boileau Arms   201 Castelnau

The name derives from the ancient house of Boileau whose seat from the beginning of the sixteenth century was at Castelnau de la Garde near Nimes in southern France. Following the revocation of the Edict of Nantes in 1685, certain members of this Huguenot family sought refuge in Britain, settling initially in Southampton, later in Dublin, and finally, from 1804, in Mortlake at Tower House, aptly renamed Castelnau Place. In due course this house passed to Charles Lestock Boileau, an army man, who on his retirement in 1839 made what must have proved a very shrewd purchase of land just south of Hammersmith Bridge. The land was developed in the form of villas (Castelnau Villas) and Castelnau came into existence. At the same time Boileau built himself a house, predictably styled Castelnau House.

The Boileau Arms Tavern - to give it its original name - is situated at the junction of Lonsdale Road and Castelnau. It dates from 1842 when, as a new building, it was recorded as licensed premises in the Barnes Vestry Minutes. The arms of Boileau de Castelnau together with the family motto De Tout Mon Coeur, were built into the west wall of the building and could be seen from the street through the gate leading into the garden of the public house.

Landlords:-

1 December	1842 - 16 May 1844	Thomas Kerfoot
17 May	1844 - 23 September 1844	Thomas Reynolds
24 September	1844 - 1 June 1846	William Swaine
2 June	1846 - 1851	James Bone
	1859 - 1860	William Packwood
	1862 - 1873	Soloman Houseman

Between 1865 and 1872 the public house was known as The Boileau Arms Tavern and Racket Ground, Lonsdale Road.

1876 - 1891	Peter Blade
1891	Mrs Mary Ann Blade (wife of the above)
1900 - 1903	James Edward Cosham
1939	A E Russell

One of its attractive features was the conservatory which ran across the back of the building and from which steps led down to a pleasant garden. Part of this is now the car park with entrance from Lonsdale Road.

The Boileau Arms, in November 1982, was owned by the Courage Brewery and was closed while extensive renovations were carried out. Its new leaseholder, Chaucer Inns, hoped to be in business by the spring. Some residents were unhappy with the plans which were afoot to change the name of the well - known landmark that had a bus stop named after it. The North Barnes Residents Association drew up a petition to oppose the change, but to no avail. Mr Alan Lubin for Chaucer Inns confirmed that they would definitely change the name from The Boileau Arms which just conjured up an image of a boozer.

A one hundred and forty year connection with the Boileau family was broken when the renovated structure with a new colonial image, was renamed The Old Rangoon in June 1983, only to be reinstated later in the 80's as The Boileau Arms.

In February 1984, The Old Rangoon was described as a flamboyant example of the theme public house. It had a tea planter clubhouse bar with an emphasis on cocktails, though there was Directors' Real Ale. Your change, should there be any, came on saucers. There was an upmarket barbecue restaurant in a conservatory setting serving lunch and dinner till midnight everyday, also afternoon set teas from 3.30 - 5.30 pm (Sunday 4.00 - 5.30 pm). A tiled terrace with pillars overlooked an enormous garden with a pond, children's playground and car park.

In November 1984, David Paul Marnane was granted a Protection Order for The Old Rangoon by the Justices. The decision meant he could trade in liquor there until the Full Brewster Session later.

Bass Taverns, who took over the ownership of The Boileau Arms, changed the name in 1995 to The Garden House.

The brewery giants, Bass, in the early months of 1999 spent over £1.5 million transforming the former Boileau Arms into a 270 seater Browns Restaurant and Bar.

The Boileau Arms - Castelnau - Barnes - c 1960

The Builders Arms   36 Railway Street

Landlord   1876 - 1878   Mr Nederick McKellar

At the Borough of Barnes Council meeting of 15 February 1939 the Town Clerk reported:-

> 1) that the Council had recently demolished certain properties in St Ann's Passage under the No. 9 Barnes (St Ann's Passage) Compulsory Purchase Order 1936 and, that on such demolition circumstances had come to light which might give occasion for the raising of questions as to the ownership of a flank wall which adjoined The Builders Arms.

> 2) that, after consultation with them a letter had been received from Messrs. Watney, Combe, Reid and Co. Ltd., dated 1 February 1939 stating that subject to the Council conveying the freehold of land on which the wall previously separated this public house from the cottages stands, and surrendering any rights which the Council have in the wall, they will agree to accept liability for it and will arrange to remove the existing plaster and projections and render the wall in cement and sand.

Resolved - that the Council convey the freehold of the land on which the wall previously separated this public house from the cottages stands, to Messrs. Watney, Combe, Reid and Co. Ltd., subject to their accepting all liability therefore, and that the Mayor be authorised to affix the Corporation seal to the document.

Clipston's Beer House / The Railway Arms / The Railway Hotel / The Red Rover / Cafe More   470 Upper Richmond Road

This public house was situated at the junction of the Upper Richmond Road and Rocks Lane and, over the years, had been known by the above names.

In July 1865 the tenants presented to the Lords of the Manor "that the beer shop lately erected in substitution of the Gatekeeper's cottage at the junction between Hammersmith Bridge Road and the Upper Richmond Road near to the Roehampton Road is an encroachment on the waste and illegal and that the tenants of the beer shop and also the tenants of the other tenements in line therewith westward and abutting on the waste northwards are in the habit of trespassing on the waste by using the same for their own purposes, such as putting on the waste, cabs, omnibuses, carts and horses, erecting posts and lines, putting drainage, dung heaps and refuse matter on the waste, and they suggest that a fence be put up to separate more effectually the beer shop and the tenements from the waste with a view to prevent trespassing."

Landlords:-   1865 - 1872   Mr John Yeoman Clipston
               1890   Mr John Lawn

It was known as The Railway Arms in 1900 when Mr Charles Henry Wynn was the landlord.

In 1929 there was a suggestion that the first roundabout in the district should be here, but this was turned down as 'likely to spoil the beauty of the common.' However, two years later traffic lights made their appearance there.

Landlord Edward Peter was followed by Mrs Louisa Rose Coe. On 9 February 1938 Mrs Coe was requested by Barnes Borough Council to prevent the display of placards by newspaper vendors on her property, and in a letter dated 15 February 1938 she stated that she had given instructions to the news - vendors not to display their placards on the fence of her premises. Mrs Coe requested that, should any future complaints arise, the Council should take action with the persons concerned on her behalf.

When it was known as The Red Rover it bore the sign of a red stage coach. The Red Rover stage coach, was acquired by Watney, Combe, Reid & Co Ltd., in 1950. It was the last stage coach to compete on a regular route served by railways, plying until 1843 between The Bolt-in-Tun, Fleet Street, since destroyed, and the Red Lion Inn, Southampton.

The licensee in 1960 at The Red Rover was A E Churchill.

The Red Rover, reopened in April 1983 after a major development aimed at improving customer facilities and service. Landlords Buck and Pauline Taylor offered customers a choice

Clipston's Beer House - Barnes - c 1869 - cross roads showing Roehampton Lane

of five traditional ales alongside which there were three different lagers and a traditional draught cider, together with traditional food.

Finally named the Cafe More, by 1997 the now derelict building had been demolished to make way for a housing development. In 1998 Bewley Homes completed the building of 3 two bedroomed houses, 4 two bedroomed flats and a one bedroomed flat, thus ending the uncertainty over the future of the former public house site. The price of the new homes ranged from £120,000 to £240,000. The development which has a car park and a tower facing on to the Upper Richmond Road is known as Barnes Gate.

The Railway Hotel - Barnes - c 1920 - Looking west along the Upper Richmond Road

The Edinburgh Castle   73 White Hart Lane

Benjamin Thorne, a brewer, who had a small brewery next to The Bulls Head on The Terrace and moved into Westfield House in 1852, supplied The Edinburgh Castle public house at the corner of Archway Street with his Thorne's Grey Horse brand of ales and stout.

Landlords:-   1870 - 03   Mr Andrew Rollo
               1876 - 84   Mrs Charlotte Eliza Rollo

The North Surrey Bicycle Association which had been formed on 26 June 1875 had their headquarters at The Edinburgh Castle, in 1876 the Honorary Secretary at that time was Mr H A Barrow of The Ferns, Barnes. Their uniform was navy blue with buff belts.

Landlords:-   1900 - 03   Mr James Henry Slater

               1939   Mr Robert Gay

The Edinburgh Castle - Barnes - c 1900 - At the corner of Archway Street and White Hart Lane

The Edinburgh Castle used to belong to the Meux's Brewery Company Ltd., which eventually became Friary Meux, brewing at Guildford, and Ind Coope Ltd took the latter over in 1964.

In February 1984 the patrons could obtain everyday public house food at lunch time and snacks were available in the evenings. There was a paved garden at the rear, whilst the interior decor was at the subdued end of the spectrum. Patrons could listen to music from a juke box or amuse themselves on the fruit machines, whilst supping their chosen tipple.

In May 1996 The Edinburgh Castle changed its name to The Tree House, following a £85,000 refurbishment to draw a more 'food orientated' customer to the premises and re-opened ahead of schedule. Rory O'Connell, the restaurant manager, said: "We actually opened the doors a few days ahead of schedule in order to give customers a sneak preview. Opening early also gave us a chance to gauge what customers wanted to see on offer and allowed us to develop our menus to suit as we plan to change them every two weeks. It is important that we are able to meet the customers' needs."

The Edinburgh Castle - Barnes - c 1960 - At the corner of Archway Street and White Hart Lane

The Kings Arms   Coles Corner

The Kings Arms was built in 1662 and stood on or near the present site of Ye White Hart at Coles Corner, which was the junction of White Hart Lane and Barnes Terrace. In 1689 Mr Charles Warner had the messuage called the Kings Arms at Coles Corner (see present pubs in Barnes).

The Market Gardener   32 Priest's Bridge

The inn sign which for many years used to hang outside this public house depicted John or Johnny Biggs, as he was called, wearing a tall black hat, sitting on his black horse and holding a glass of ale in his right hand.

Landlords :-   1860 - 63   Penston
                1865 - 67   Mrs Ann Penston
                1882   Mr John Crow
                1891   Mrs Mary Ann Crow   Owner Watson Farnell
                1900 - 02   Mr Thomas Bacon
                1903   Mrs Charlotte Bacon

                1960   Mr G R Dudding

In February 1984 there were two separate bars to this Watney public house. The saloon bar, at that time, was papered with notable newspaper stories and led through to a small patio, whilst the patrons of the public bar could amuse themselves at the dart board, pool table or play dominoes. At this time The Market Gardener had a darts team, but as yet no records of whom they played against or their results have been discovered.

Landlords :-   1985   Mr Brian Courtice
                1991   Miss Ellen Rochford

Lunch time drinkers were marooned in The Market Gardener on Saturday 23 November 1991 after a three foot diameter mains water pipe burst, sending gallons of water cascading through its doors, and several elderly people had to be carried through the deep water.

The Market Gardeners - Priest Bridge - Barnes - From a drawing by Albert Betts - 1893

The Market Gardeners - Priest Bridge - Barnes - showing a delivery of Royal Stout

Landlady, Ellen Rochford, described the scene by saying "It was like that beer advert except there was no man on the surfboard. There was no warning, the water just came gushing in." Much of the public house stayed under water until the following day.

Staff were forced to cancel a string of functions after beer was contaminated by four feet of water which flooded through the bar, flooding the cellar and ruining carpets.

Latterly known as The Maggot and Maybe it closed its doors to the public in 1998. The building, which had been boarded up, was demolished during the early part of the year 2000, and a planning application has been made by Mr Norman Ullathorne of Petersham Road, Richmond to build four flats and two three storey houses on the site.

The Market Gardeners - Priest Bridge - Barnes - c 1920 - This roadway was known as Hoggers Corner

The Rayne Deer Barnes Waterfront

An inn standing on or near the site of the present Bulls Head on the Barnes Waterfront is mentioned as early as 1649 when Thomas Reeve was admitted as tenant to a messuage known by "the signe of The Rayne Deer." On 4 June 1672 the Rayne Deer is referred to as The Kings Head, when R Ash was the proprietor (see present pubs in Barnes).

The Rose Barnes High Street

The Rose dated from the time of Charles I; the top floor of the inn may well have been used as a dormitory probably by watermen who manned the barges on the river. In 1663 Marjory Gibson, possibly the late landlord's widow, surrendered a messuage or tenement called Ye sign of The Rose at the Manor Court. At some time in the eighteenth century the inn became a private dwelling house known as Rose House. Saved from demolition in 1974 it is currently the headquarters of the Barnes Community Association.

Rose House - 70 Barnes High Street - 17th century with 18th, 19th and 20th century additions - Listed Grade 11 building - Head Quarters of Barnes Community Association which owns the building

The Three Cups Tavern   Barnes High Street

The Three Cups Tavern no longer exists, it appears to have been no more than a small beerhouse which in 1890 was occupied by Edward Basten. It was stated that this property had previously been two cottages numbered 37 and 38 High Street Barnes when Benjamin Thomas Wright and William Saddler acquired the interest of the Lord of the Manor in a coffee tavern, by a deed of enfranchisement dated 27 July 1899.

The Watermans Arms   Lonsdale Road

In the seventeenth and eighteenth centuries a number of Barnes men are recorded as Barge masters or Watermen. In one of the two cottages next to a blacksmith's shop there lived in the first half of the nineteenth century the last of the Watermen in the place, named William Hill. He had a brother Henry, but he was more frequently employed on barge work as a lighterman. Hill let out boats for hire, and went every day to London in a wherry to carry goods backwards and forwards for the inhabitants. On Hill's death no one took up the business, which had already died out.

The Watermans Arms was a reminder of this one-time important local occupation, standing opposite the site of a former landing stage.

In 1837 the site on which The Watermans Arms was built was held in copyhold by Mrs Elizabeth Biggs. At that time there were two customary cottages or tenements and shop (formally used by a blacksmith's shop) and backside adjoining each other "situate lying and being within the Manor of Barnes fronting West to the river Thames East and North on a public house and premises called the Bulls Head and South on Barnes Street formerly in the possession of Richard Phillips and since Emanuel Lavonsky and John Head."

The Watermans Arms was enfranchised by Anne Miller on 22 July 1880. The land then consisted of "a newly erected messuage or tenement and premises used as a beer house or public house late in the occupation of James Griffen but now known as the Watermans Arms and in the occupation of Henry Bowyer 1860 - 1878."

Landlords:-		
		Mr John Fisher
	1889	Mr Arthur Levett
	1900	Mr John Abbott
		Mr Thomas George Green
		Mr Thomas Mason
	1939	Mrs S Mason

In February 1984 this was a friendly unpretentious public house where conversation and darts were the main activities, though there was a jukebox.

Landlord:-   1987   Mr W J Hutchinson

Closed 2 April 1988 and reopened December 1988 after a refurbishment.

Now the site of the Caffe Uno.

ERALD Barnes & Mortlake Herald. 1953.

There's a different aspect to-day at this junction of Lonsdale-road and Barnes High-street. They were better off in the days when this picture was taken in the matter of transport than we are to-day. They had the horse bus between Hammersmith and Barnes, which is seen standing at what was the terminus. So much do we want transport along Lonsdale-road as the repeated applications to the London Transport Executive indicate that we would not turn up our noses at a horse bus.

This picture was taken before the police station was built in Lonsdale-road and it was at the time when the corn boats used to come with their cargo to the little jetty just visible for Woods, the corn chandlers. It was also the time, too, before the river wall. And there was no need for a zebra crossing in those days.

Here is a note for Barnes Council. We are strong supporters of the Swans for Barnes Pond Movement and referred to it with last week's picture of the Pond. We have been surprised at the support of the public for the movement. Many people have asked that we keep up the agitation for a pair of swans to be put on the Pond. They say, like us, that the Pond without swans does not seem like the Pond at all. The solution is with you Barnes Council.

The Beare   Site Unknown

In 1635 The Beare appears to have been a tavern of some importance with "barnes, stables and other premises" which were kept by Richard Hill. Henry Day relinquished The Beare in 1665, the year the great plague carried off twenty three people in the village of Barnes. In the seventeenth century, Charles Goodwin, vintner of Barnes, issued his tokens inscribed on the obverse "Charles Goodwin - His Half Peny" and on the reverse "of Barnes Vintner" - around the figure of a bear.

Map of East Sheen showing the location of the past public houses

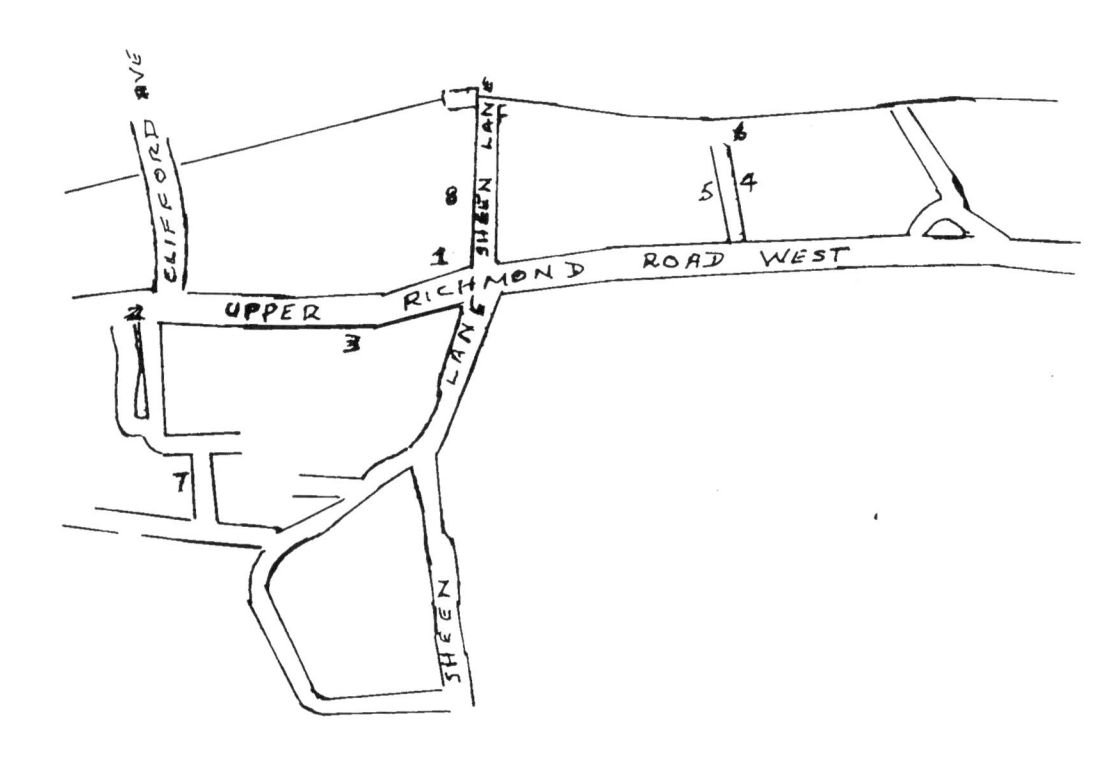

1	Bull	2	Derby Arms	3	Five Alls
4	Hand and Flower	5	Queens Arms	6	Spur
7	The Victoria	8	Wheatsheaf		

East Sheen S W 14

The Bull   262 Upper Richmond Road West

Only a few minutes walk from the Mortlake Brewery stood one of the rare old coaching houses that had not been reconstructed to any great extent prior to 1937. It is not clear when The Bull was first established, but the original sign bore the date 1696. The old coaching house stood in the middle of a row of houses known as Clarence Row which were built in 1792 and were later converted into shops. Those on the corner of Sheen Lane were pulled down in 1930 and the remainder were demolished with the coaching house in 1937, when a new Bull Hotel was erected and stood for another fifty years.

The Licensed Victuallers Recognizances (1785 - 1827) record that from 1785 - 1800 Mr Thomas Gurr was the landlord and he was succeeded by his widow Elizabeth Gurr as landlady from 1801 - 1804.

From 26 June 1794 and for upwards of five weeks not less than nine men and ten horses belonging to the Eleventh Regiment of Light Dragoons were quartered and billeted at The Bull, which at that time had twelve regular standings.

Landlords:-

1818 - 1821	Mr Thomas Gouldsmith	1822	Mr William Blundell
1823	Mr William Dean	1826 - 1839	Mr John Hammond

The rate book of 25 November 1836 records that Messrs Halford and Topham were the owners of The Bull, and their landlady from 1840 - 1841 was Mrs Elizabeth Hammond.

The rate book of 4 August 1842 records that Kempson and Topham were the owners of The Bull, and that their landlords were from 1842 - 1843 Mr Thomas Downing and from 1843 Mr Aaron Lambert Hall.

Sometime during 1851 Elizabeth Streater Halford of Vineyard House, Richmond surrendered absolutely for £1,530 to Mr George Streater Kempson:- "All that customary messuage or tenement with several stables, garden, orchard and yard thereto belonging and situate in East Sheen in the Parish of Mortlake, formerly in the occupation of John Lorton, afterwards John Richardson, and Thomas Browne, since then of Elizabeth Gurr, widow, then of Elizabeth Hammond, widow, and now or late of Aaron Hall and known by the sign of The Bull. Premises:- Bull public house with yards, gardens, stables, coach houses, sheds, wash house, skittle ground and including Clarence Row and Clarence Cottages."

Landlords:-

    1855 - 1856   Mr W Garter
    1857   Mr Walter Easter
    1860 - 1867   Mr Henry Bailey

The rate book of 15 May 1863 records that Phillips and Wigan were the owners of The Bull, and that their landlords were from 1868 Mr W Morris, 1872 Mr Joseph W Hagger and from 1882 - 1890 Mrs Elizabeth Hagger.

The rate book of 10 June 1891 records that Watney & Co. were the owners of The Bull, and that their landlord was from 1891 - 1903 Mr Charles Fisher.

At sometime during 1937 the only four - horse stage coach running daily in the world during the season, called at The Bull, where the horses were changed, fed and watered in the original stables at the rear of the premises. The coach was the "Greyhound" and it operated from The Berkeley Hotel, Piccadilly, via Hammersmith to Hampton Court.

Time had begun to tell upon this old house and after many designs had been made plans were finally approved and the builders took possession in 1937 and the process of demolition commenced. The existing house, several adjoining shops, cottages and stabling were pulled down to be replaced by a large modern house, with restaurant and entertainment facilities necessitated by the district.

The site was exceedingly difficult for it had frontages to both the Upper Richmond Road West and Sheen Lane, but did not include the corner building, a bank. The new building therefore had to be designed to encircle the bank, and to provide a large courtyard and car park at the

The Bull and Clarence Row - Upper Richmond Road - East Sheen - c 1900 - The old coaching house in the middle of a row of houses known as Clarence Row which were built in 1792

rear of the premises, with entrances from both Upper Richmond Road West and Sheen Lane. The finished design was a great credit to Mr A W Blomfield, FRIBA, the architect, and his drawings of the frontages to the Upper Richmond Road West and the courtyard in Sheen Lane were exhibited at the Royal Academy summer exhibitions respectively in 1937 and 1938.

The Bull public house at the junction of Upper Richmond Road West and Sheen Lane, was for many years the centre of the district's municipal and political life. In fact, the large first floor room, the Penrhyn Rooms, so named after a well - known family who at one time owned a large part of Sheen and Mortlake, was used as a council chamber by the old Barnes Borough Council, after its previous meeting place was bombed during the Second World War. It was also used for the annual meetings of the Richmond and Barnes Conservative Association during the time when the number of Liberal supporters in the area could have been counted on one hand - or maybe two!

One of the difficulties that newspaper reporters had to contend with when the Council met at The Bull was the noise of passing traffic, particularly in the summer months when the windows were open. Many words uttered by Council members failed to be recorded for posterity - because no-one ever heard them. It was better in winter, when the windows were shut, but it was also the practice of the public house in the 1950's and 1960's to provide piped music - if it could be called music - to the public house's innumerable rooms, including the first floor room where the Council met.

The Mayoral chair, incidentally, was kept in the gentlemen's cloakroom except during the twelve months when a woman Mayor presided over the almost comical meetings of the authority, then it was kept in the ladies' cloakroom.

The Bull and Clarence Row - Upper Richmond Road - East Sheen - c 1903 - From a drawing by W Lewis Turner

The Bull and Clarence Row - Upper Richmond Road - East Sheen - c 1936 - The old coaching house and part of a row of houses known as Clarence Row converted into shops

During the summer of 1981 the owners Watney's in conjunction with the new lessee, Mr Sean McCormack, carried out renovation and refurbishment to the public house to include a carvery and a la carte restaurant, buffet room, ballroom and at the rear a gazebo ideal for photographs of a bride and groom holding their reception at the public house. The pseudo flying buttresses to the front elevation came under severe criticism from many local people who felt that the new look just did not blend with the surroundings.

The ugly protuberances which looked like sawn off flying buttresses under the fascia of The Bull, and which aroused much unfavourable comment when first put up, were removed. At the same time the name of the public house was repainted in handsome gilt Roman capitals with black outline and the etceteras below appeared in a splendid copperplate script.

In February 1983 The Bull came under the new management of Mr and Mrs Dean, who had recently returned after ten years in the United States. Amid much redecoration, G & W Catering took over with an imaginative food angle. The Bull's Smithfield carvery room was a must, it was here that you could buy for £4.95 a three course cooked-while-you-wait meal, including freshly made farmhouse soup, roast Scotch beef, with roast potatoes, Yorkshire pudding and seasonal fresh vegetables. Another attraction was that of David Prideaux, who was the resident pianist every Tuesday, Thursday and Saturday.

During March 1983 Malc Murphy's Storyville Quartet were to be found playing New Orleans style jazz every Sunday evening from 8.15 to 10.30 in the Lounge bar.

In June 1984 the Managing Director of Mecca Speciality Leisure, Mr R. Zanre, was working on plans to give The Bull a new look, but would not reveal any details beyond that the ground floor area would probably be run on pub and restaurant lines – something really interesting and exciting. He also said "there were no plans to change the banqueting reception and public - meeting facilities and that regulars should have no cause for concern – given that the Bull had stood there as an inn for over three hundred years."

PHEASANT PLUCKERS WANTED
for our
Pleasant Pheasant Night
AT
THE BULL AT SHEEN

THURS., 1st DECEMBER, 1983

£12.95 + Service Charge
FUN NIGHT WITH MUSIC
MENU
Farmhouse Soup (Walton Style), Pheasant (Chef's Garnish), Lyonnaise Potatoes, Minted Peas, Baked Parsnips, Cointreau Trifle, Coffee & Mints.
Reservations now being taken
TELEPHONE 01-876 2345/6964
262 Upper Richmond Road West
East Sheen SW14

Christmas Festivities
AT
THE BULL AT SHEEN

GRAND CHRISTMAS EVE AND NEW YEAR'S EVE DINNER DANCE
LIVE MUSIC
THAMES T.V. DANCE BAND
TICKETS £9.00 PER HEAD
Reservations now being taken
MAGICIAN NEW YEAR'S EVE
Fancy Dress :: ★PRIZES★
262 Upper Richmond Rd. West
East Sheen SW14

The new manager of The Bull at Sheen is determined to make full use of the grand facilities available there. The manager, Francis De Laat, has had more than 10 years international catering experience and has already put into practice many of his clever ideas. Christmas and New Year are bound to be good fun, with a "Pheasant Pluckers" dinner planned! Tel. 876 6964 for reservations.

Barnes, Mortlake and Sheen Times
Friday November 18 1983

Here endeth the history of The Bull at Shene for during the week commencing 16 January 1987 the demolition contractors began clearing out the interior of the building before moving their equipment onto the site in preparation to knock down the existing structures for complete redevelopment. This would comprise a block of three large shops fronting the Upper Richmond Road West together with a new public house with flats over in Sheen Lane. This is believed to have cost one and a quarter million pounds and the brewery Watney, Combe, Reid will remain the freeholders.

All that remains of The Bull, the well-known landmark at East Sheen town centre. Watneys are planning to erect a new pub on the site.

The Derby Arms   565 Upper Richmond Road West

The Derby Arms was situated on the south side of the Upper Richmond Road West at the corner with Stanley Road. It was established in the last quarter of the nineteenth century and must have been much frequented by the market garden workers from the opposite side of the road. It derived its name, as do the roads between which it stood, from Lady Charlotte Penrhyn of The Cedars, East Sheen, who was the sister of Edward Stanley, Earl of Derby.

The present three storey building with a mansard roof, was built in the late 1920's on a site behind the earlier building.

Landlords:-   1884   Mr Robert Thomas Towler
               1885   Mr Harry Symonds Hartnell

The Mortlake rate book of 10 June 1891 states that Watney & Co are the owners and Mr George Ellis is the landlord.

Landlords:-   1899 - 1900   Mr Samuel George Brown
               1928   Mr Edward George Warwick
               1939   Mr Thomas Charles and Mrs Dorothy Alice Potter

In 1960 the landlord was Mr Len Harvey, who had previously been a well known light heavy weight boxer. Taking over a public house for the first time, thirty eight year old Mr Ted Fenge moved into The Derby Arms as licensee in October 1962.

Between April 1966 and October 1970 the landlord was Mr Frank Westby.

The Derby Arms - Upper Richmond Road - East Sheen - near Derby Road. From a drawing by W Lewis Turner 1903

In June 1982 Jayne and Robbie Clausen announced their arrival as hosts at The Derby Arms with an advert in the "Richmond Informer", which read "In order to welcome old and new friends, regular happy hours will be held throughout July from 7 to 8 pm. Special offers will include – Wine by the glass at fifty pence, Fosters lager at fifty five pence a pint and Jayne's superb cuisine specially prepared to complement these. Pool, darts and video screen music will be available in the public bar while the saloon bar facilities include a garden patio and barbecue. On Friday and Saturday there will be live entertainment, whilst the extensive function room facilities on the first floor will be available for weddings and private parties at very reasonable rates."

Landowners Grand Metropolitan Estates, who called time on drinkers in 1987, have a number of public houses in the area and deemed The Derby Arms "surplus to requirements." A lack of popularity and a series of violent incidents, which had led to no possible tenants coming forward to take over the public house, together with a lack of parking space may have contributed to their decision.

The Derby Arms - Upper Richmond Road - East Sheen - Reproduced by kind permission of Courage - The building has now been converted into flats

In January 1989 The Derby Arms was turned into nine flats. The shell and some of the original features have been retained in the construction of 7 two bedroom and 2 three bedroom apartments with off street parking, and were sold at prices between £110,000 and £130,000.

The Five Alls   Upper Richmond Road West

This beer house once stood in a row of cottages on The Cedars Estate between Penrhyn Crescent and Sheen Gate Gardens and was pulled down in 1934 to make way for shops.

The name "Five Alls" is a curious inn sign and means :- I pray for all (a clergyman), I plead for all (a barrister), I maintain all (a farmer with a sickle in his hand), I fight for all (a king with a sword in his hand), I take all (his satanic majesty).

Mr Bowling intended becoming the landlord, but the licence was taken away for some offence against the law and it ultimately became the property of Mr E Hugh Leycester Penrhyn.

Woodbine Cottage - Five Alls - c 1930 - Upper Richmond Road - East Sheen

The Hand and Flower   Queens Road

The landlord of this beer house in 1871 was Mr Thomas Jackman, who was also a carpenter. He was followed in 1872 by Mr Thomas Collins. In 1895 the landlady was Mrs Emily Lovett.

The Queens Arms   3 Princes Road

Landlords:-   1872   Mr Charles Lindsey
              1882   Mr Edgar Bourne
              1890 - 91   Mrs Emily Bourne

Landlord:-   1960   T A Murrell

In February 1984, this public house with its brown glazed - tiled exterior and tinted leaded windows, was a community public house with an admixture of London transport personnel, which at that time was tucked away in a workman's cottage enclave which has much come up of late. The patrons could amuse themselves on a fruit machine, listen to music played on the piano or play darts. The Queens Arms at this time had a darts team, but as yet no records of who they played against or their results have been discovered.

Strangers visiting this public house in 1987 could be forgiven for feeling that they recognised a face behind the bar as tenant, Terry Horan, looked so much like actor Sean Connery that he had been used as his double in some of the James Bond films.

The public house, at this time had mostly a local clientele including some celebrities of stage and screen. It had a nice homely feel to the place, with its wooden panelling, low ceiling and floral - patterned pottery on the walls and shelves. There were also old prints on the walls of the property's single large bar.

It was reported in the local press in December 1997 that houses could replace the empty public house more than a year after last orders were called at the bar, as developers wanted to convert the Queens Arms into two family houses and a cottage. The two storey Victorian property, a Building of Townscape Merit, had been on the market for a year before the scheme was submitted to Richmond Council. Neighbours objected to the plans, claiming that it would cause parking problems and was too big for the Conservation Area whilst others said it would block out light and would overlook their houses. There were also fears that historic chimneys would be demolished.

It was reported in the local press that the Queens Arms would be demolished to make way for four houses including a two storey cottage, despite strong opposition from local residents anxious to preserve the picturesque building.

The Queens Arms - Princes Road - East Sheen - 1969

The Spur   36 South Worple Way

The Spur public house which once stood at the corner of South Worple Way and Queens Road was popularly held to be named from the adjacent railway footbridge, but the Spur Bridge, as it is called, of rare design, dates only from 1903 when it replaced a foot level crossing, whereas The Spur itself belonged to the 1860's.

The story behind the beerhouse is fairly complicated. The Spur was erected by Charles (or Charley) Smith, one time coachman to Dr John Scott of the Angles, a house which stood near Wayside, off Sheen Lane. Dr. Scott's only daughter by his first wife (a Miss Boileau) married Mr John Johnson, who won the Derby with a horse called "Pretender". The Spur beerhouse was called after Johnson's crest which was a "spur".

Smith remained in service with Mrs Scott when the doctor died and when he built the public

The Spur - South Worple Way - East Sheen - c 1904 - From a drawing by W Lewis Turner

The Spur - South Worple Way - East Sheen - Reproduced by kind permission of Courage

The Spur - South Worple Way - East Sheen - 1969

house he named it The Spur, out of compliment . But Smith's contribution to local naming did not end there. As the cottages around The Spur were built, a friend asked him what he was going to call the development. At that time there was a hit song, "Let's all go down to Charlestown" and since Smith's name was Charles, the name Charlestown was suggested. That is the story, but in 1860, the Vestry, the local Authority of the day, gave the name official status. And a few years later Charlestown appeared on the map. The name is still used by older residents and those in the know. Charlestown comprises Queens Road, Princes Road, Kings Road, Lodge Avenue, Rock Avenue and Treherne Road.

The rate book of 15 May 1863 records the owner as Smith and the landlord as Cook.

Landlords:-		
	1863 - 1867	Mr Matthew Cook
	1872	Mr William Agate
	1876	Mr Joseph Richardson
	1878	Mr R H Kettley
	1882	Mrs Mary Baker
	1884	Bishop Sampson
	1890	Mrs Eliza Newton

The rate book of 10 June 1891 records the owner as Watney & Co. and the landlord is William John Wilde.

Landlady:-	1982	Mrs Cathy Wright

In February 1984, in one of the bars the patrons could amuse themselves at the pool table or play darts. Whilst a recent conversion to the other bars left the Swiss cottage mini roof floating over the patrons.

The Spur public house was demolished towards the end of May and the beginning of June 1995, and a block of four terraced two storey houses were built on the site.

The Victoria   10 West Temple Sheen

The Victoria was probably built somewhere between 1845 and 1855 when East Sheen consisted largely of three estates. Most of the customers, at that time, would probably have been the people from 'downstairs' on the estates – butlers, footmen and coachmen.

The Victoria is situated not far from Richmond Park and Sheen Common, and inside the country public house atmosphere was enhanced in the 1980's by tapestry furnishings and the lovingly polished wood bar.

The rate book of 31 May 1855 and 15 May 1863 state that Farnell is the owner of The Victoria.

Landlords:-			
	31 May	1855	Bell
	22 November	1855	Mr William Turner
	12 June	1856	Mr George Turner

The Victoria - West Temple Sheen - East Sheen - From a drawing by W Lewis Turner - 1904

In 1860, Mr George Turner is described in the Post Office London Suburban Directory for that year as being a beer retailer, however, in the 1862 Directory, he is stated as being at The Victoria and remained until 1866. In 1867 Mrs G Turner is recorded as the landlady, whilst in 1868 it is Mrs E Turner.

   1872 - 1890 Mr Henry Aubrey

Mr Watson Farnell was the owner at this time.

   1936 - 1939 Mr Jas George Littlewood

Mr and Mrs J E Firman, who had run The Victoria for the past twenty four years, retired on Tuesday 27 January 1976 to the quiet village of Rushington in Sussex. Having been at The Victoria for such a long time the couple could remember when current regular customers were simply babies in the pram, brought to the public house by their parents, "Now they have got their own children." Before they took over The Victoria, Mr and Mrs Firman had run a public house in Kingston, but they claimed The Victoria had its own special atmosphere. "There is no other place like it in terms of clientele and atmosphere. It is so countrified, with a lovely garden, and we enjoyed every minute" said 67 year old Mr Firman who was known to the regulars as Ted.

THE VICTORIA
10 West Temple Sheen,
EAST SHEEN, SW14
Tel: 876 4238

We are now offering extensive pub lunches, 7 days a week. Also evening grills, including steaks, gammon, chicken and hamburgers *every* night of the week until 10.15pm (Sunday 9.45pm).

A WARM WELCOME AWAITS YOU

in a friendly atmosphere, offering a good selection of wines and real ales (including Ruddles County and WEBSTERS YORKSHIRE BITTER). And don't forget our Happy 2 H evening (except Sunda or vodka) at only £1 a York

Richmond & Twickenham Informer Thursday October 18 1984

Pub extension

A FAMILY pub in East Sheen is to build an extension for bed and breakfast facilities.

The Victoria on West Temple Sheen submitted plans for a two storey rear extension and first floor rear extension which wil ahead subject to the c granting permission.

Barnes, Mortlake & Sheen Times Friday January 30 1998

EAST SHEEN
Victoria Public House, West Temple Sheen Extensions to provide additional bedrooms for bed and breakfast service (97/2585/ful Sheen); 64-66 Stanley Road Brick and glass building over swimming pool (98/62/ful Sheen).

A change for the better at T' Victoria Public House

UNDER new management since the end of August 1998, The Victoria Public House, West Temple Sheen has certainly been witness to some changes.

Re-decorated, with a new team of staff and an extensive new menu; the pub has been slowly drawing back customers who had stopped frequenting it years ago.

The new management team, Bob and Jan Butterworth are determined to put the pub firmly back on the local map and have already become well respected locally for the good home-cooked food and wide variety of drink the pub offers its customers.

The Victoria has also been taking advantage of its stunning conservatory by filling it with hungry customers at weekends, hiring it out privately for special occasions and using it as a venue for a range of successful musical evenings. Several opera duos, string quartets and choirs have recently entertained customers enjoying a delicious four-course gourmet dinner.

The Victoria Public House in West Temple, Sheen. Telephone 0181 876 4238.

Barnes, Mortlake & Sheen Times Friday January 23 1998

Barnes, Mortlake & Sheen Times Friday March 12 1999

Whilst cleaning the basement of The Victoria, Mr Michael Fisher, a Watney Director, found two handsome terracotta busts of a remarkably young looking Albert and Victoria and the busts took pride of place in the quiet local run by tenants John and Edna Newall. Mr and Mrs Newall had run two public houses before, one in Heston and the other in Addlestone, but "after twenty years in the business this is the sort of place that we've looked forward to running."

In 1981 for the third time running the licensees John and Edna Newall won the Watney Inn - keepers London West Floral Competition, becoming Champion of Champions. They were first in the garden and floral sections of the competition for their displays both at the front of the public house and for the public house garden. A record number of sixty-six public houses entered the competition which was judged by Mr John Ottoway from the Royal Hospital Gardens in Chelsea, Jacqueline Kettell, wife of Watney's London Managing Director (trading) and Don Scott, a retired surveyor from Watneys London. Their prizes were the Champion of Champions cup for the best overall winners and trips to Paris and Miami.

David and Maggie Kolmar took over the tenancy of The Victoria in April 1982 - their first for Watneys London. As part of the refurbishment programme, the bar area was extended, a food servery installed and the kitchen area refitted and re-equipped. The public house was redecorated throughout, with new carpets, curtains and furniture. In addition a car park was built at the rear of the property.

The Victoria closed its doors to the public during June 2000 and opened as a restaurant in September of that year.

Barnes, Mortlake & Sheen Times
Friday March 12 1999

Barnes, Mortlake & Sheen Times
Friday May 7 1999

The Wheatsheaf   Sheen Lane

With the demolition of The Wheatsheaf, long since benign and defunct in Sheen Lane, a celebrated link with a Mortlake of harder times disappeared for ever. In the days when drunkenness and poverty were as often as not common partners, it represented for those who sought it a haven of happiness and well - being for as long as the money lasted. To local temperance workers and others interested in what was called "the welfare of the working classes," it was little more than a veritable house of sin.

Such was its reputation for violence and intemperance in its Victorian heyday that "respectable" people, wishing to proceed from Mortlake village to the upper road, would often go by way of Church Path, which crossed the railway and continued obliquely through Portobello fields, rather than run the gauntlet of Sheen Lane at the point where The Wheatsheaf stood like a citadel at the entrance to Hampton Square.

According to a document dated 23 May 1857, which together with a number of magnificently scrivened deeds and legal instruments relating to The Wheatsheaf, held at one time by Barnes Borough Council, the premises were erected by Mr Charles Harvey of Mortlake. But the exact age of the building must remain in doubt, because an indenture made of 9 May the same year between James Hampton of Shepherd's Bush and one William Lipscombe, relates to a lease for ninety - five years, less two days, to commence from three years earlier, 29 September 1854.

The occupier and leaseholder of The Wheatsheaf is given in the electoral register for 1863 - 1864 as Charles Harvey, mentioned above. By 1879, when the licence was held by Jane Hester, the reputation of The Wheatsheaf spread far beyond the parish boundaries. A journalist who was attracted thither by its notoriety and the chance of a good story in October of that year, returned unscathed to the security of his editorial office and later wrote:
"....... More than half the unseemly wrangles, the violent assaults, the horrid threats and the offences generally which occupy the attention of the Richmond Magistrates seem to come from the back of The Wheatsheaf .... Leaving the train at Mortlake station and passing up Sheen Lane I came to a turning on the right - hand side, at one corner of which was a beer house, and not far off there stood a group of ragged, dirty and disreputable-looking women, who at midday seemed to have nothing better to do than stand with sleeves tucked up, hair roughly twisted in a knot and faces that had probably not been washed that day and gossiping in a loud tone of voice with their neighbours. Glancing up at the sign of the beer house I saw that it was indeed The Wheatsheaf and that I had no reason to doubt it, for it could be seen at a glance that the place was as disreputable as it had been described."

The succession of landlords at The Wheatsheaf for the remainder of the Victorian era included Mr John Breach (1879 - 1882), Mr George Dale (1886), Mr George Rowson (1887 - 1891), Mr Venner (paid £150 to take over, but died nine months afterwards), Mrs Venner (1894), Mr Joseph Hayes (1894 - 1895).

Statement of the Settlement at the **Wheatsheaf, Mortlake.** Twenty third day of September 1938

Mr. **Frederick John Wood** to Mr. **Reginald Harper Edwards**

Deductions Per Annum								
	Premium	Edwards deposited £150 @ 4% int.						
	Valuation	Co. purchased Fixtures £109.13.0 Loose Goods.				143	4	0
	License						14	8
	Insurance: Building	}						
	Ditto Stock and Goods					1	3	2
	Ditto Plate Glass							
	½ Stamp and Expenses					1	1	0
	Beer Stock					85	17	5
	British and Foreign					–	–	–
	Rates + Water paid to 30 Sept. 1938.						17	4
	Performing Rights Society. £1.1.0 p.a. paid to 5 Nov. 1938.						2	6
					Proportion.	233	3	1
	Deposit		25	0	0			
	Rent							
	Inhabited House Duty							
	Income Tax, Sch. A							
	Income Tax, Sch. A excess		3	16	10			
	Income ,, Sch. D							
	Land ,,							
	Poor Rates							
	General Rates							
	Water ,,							
	Gas							
	Odd Days Rent, Rates and Taxes							
	Notices			7	6			
			29	4	4	29	4	4
						203	18	9

Fleuret Haskell + Co. between

The Wheatsheaf - Sheen Lane - East Sheen - c 1914/20

The Wheatsheaf from 1895 until 1941 was owned by Hodgson's Kingston Brewery Co. Ltd. and their landlords were Mr James Holmes (1895 - 1913), Mr Stephen Stone (23 April - 9 December 1913). Mr Thomas Dixon took over The Wheatsheaf on 10 December 1913 and left on 11 May 1920 to take over at The Plough, he was followed by Mr Joseph Michael O'Brien (12 May 1920 - 24 March 1925), Mr Frederick John Wood (25 March 1925 - 2 September 1938), Mr Reginald Haspur Edwards (3 September 1938 - 4 December 1939), Mr H A Riley (5 December 1939 - 1940), and Mr Percy James Hornes (1940 - 1941).

From 1941 until 1949 the landlady was Mrs Florence Richards, who was succeeded by Mr Edward Bland (1957), followed by Mr Harold Johnson from June 1962, until the house finally closed its doors on Sunday 15 July of that year. During the whole of its trading life The Wheatsheaf was never licensed for the sale of spirits, although a wine licence was granted in 1953.

Watney purchased the Freehold in September 1933, subject to the lease from September 1854. Out of the 1854 lease a holding was granted to Hodgson's Kingston Brewery, and the house remained in their trade until the lease expired in 1949, after which it passed into Watney's trade. The Borough of Barnes purchased the Freehold in August 1962. The building was demolished in 1963.

The Wheatsheaf - Sheen Lane - East Sheen - 1963 - Looking south - Demolition of The Wheatsheaf has begun

The Dogge   Site Unknown

From the Survey of Mortlake in 1617:-

"Above Strat Furlong ran along the south side of the upper road from Priest Bridge to Sheen Green at this intersection of the upper road and Sheen Lane. At this corner stood a tenement and other buildings new erected beinge the sign of The Dogge, a victualling house." This property which belonged to Mr Richard Glascock contained nearly four acres and was bound on the south by Pale Lane, 'East Sheyne Street'. Its western boundary would be the southern continuation of Sheen Lane, and the presence of houses there doubtless acted as a deterrent to the agents of Charles I when enclosing the Park for his royal pleasure. This may explain the modest remoteness of the present Sheen Gate.

John Eustace Anderson in his book *Mortlake Memories* refers to The Dogge thus:-

Col. Ommanney said he heard that before The Hare and Hounds was built, there used to be a small public house opposite called The Dog, and in consequence the small gate to the north west side of Dunkley's Field, leading to the footpath across to Palewell, was called 'The Dog Gate.'

Anderson makes a further reference to The Dogge in *Sheen House Mortlake and its Inhabitants, 1898* as follows:-

> And also, all that one customary tenement called 'The Dog', (perhaps a beer house), with barn curtilages, garden, orchard and close containing four acres, with appurtenances, late in the occupation of Thomas Plow situate and being at or near 'the dog gate' (where this is I do not know) in East Sheen in the Parish of Mortlake, within the said Manor.

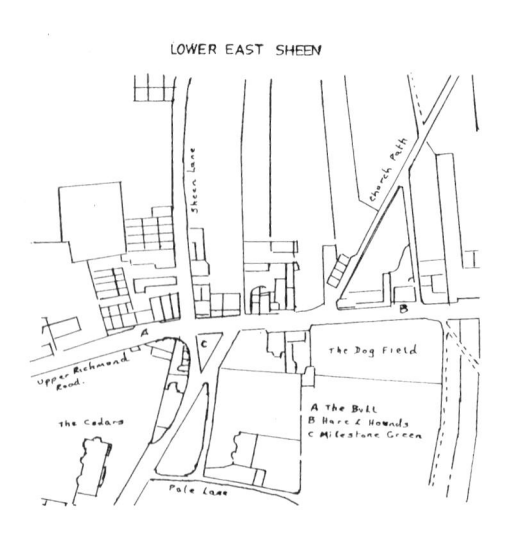

Map of Mortlake showing the location of the past public houses

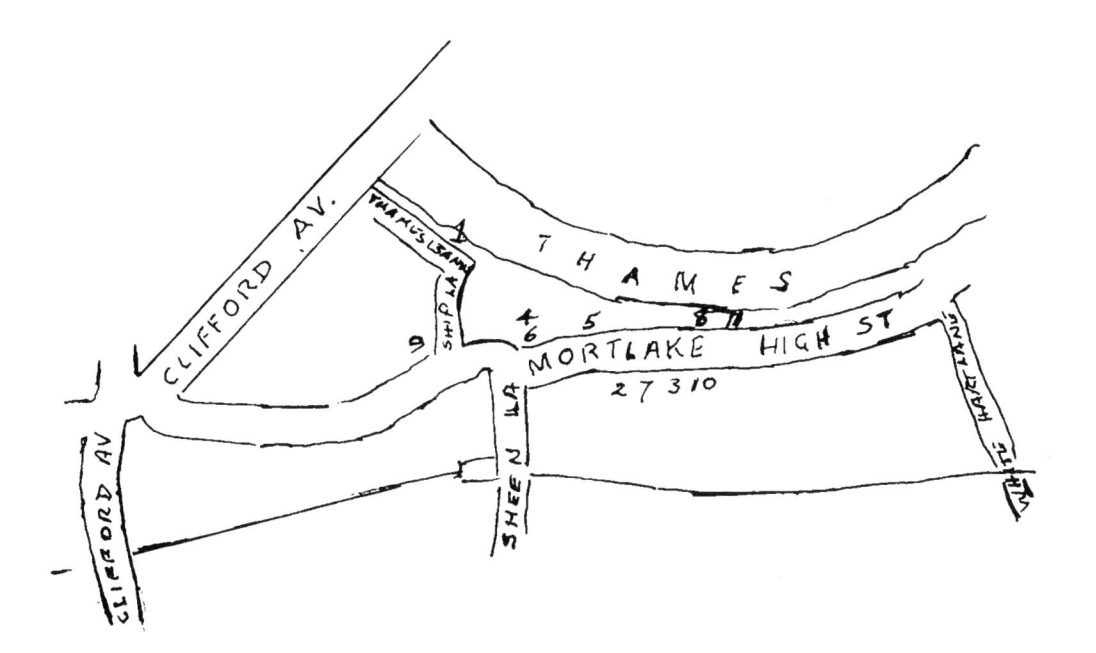

1   Ye Garter   2   The Hope   3   Jolly Maltman
4   Kings Arms   5   Lord Napier   6   Mortlake Hotel
7   Old George   8   Queens Head   9   Three Tuns
10 Two Brewers   11 Whitworth Arms

Mortlake S W 14

Ye Garter / Ye Royall Garter / Star and Garter   The Causeway

A very old house mentioned in the earliest parish records, Ye Garter / Ye Royall Garter / Star and Garter is another of Mortlake's ancient ale houses which no longer exists. It is difficult to imagine, as one walks along Thames Bank today and watches the river flowing by with very little activity on it, that river ale houses such as this thrived to serve as the main source of hospitality for those not only travelling, but also those whose livelihood depended on the river.

In 1664/5 Mr Robert Warner was charged £1:10:0 rent for Ye Royall Garter. This was a considerably large sum of money because in that year a halfpenny would buy a pint of milk, or two yards of land. Whilst the cost of employing a youth was six pence per day and an adult one shilling a day which may well have meant working a twelve hour day and would have included Saturday and perhaps part of Sunday.

From 1666 to 1679 Mr Peter White was in occupation and at sometime during this period he issued his halfpenny tokens, which were inscribed on the obverse with the issuers name 'Peter D White in Moreclake' around the man-and-wife triad of initials W over PD. The legend continues on the reverse to say 'Honi-Soit-Qui-Mal-Y-Pense' which is the motto of "The Order of the Garter" around the Arms of the City of London. From 1673 to 1676 he also held the office of Churchwarden.

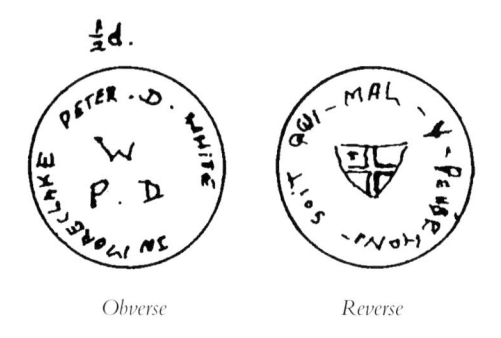

Obverse   *Reverse*

Other known occupants include from 1679 to 1682 Mrs White, 1682 to 1688 Mr Holden, 1688 to 1699 Mrs Dorothy Holden, and 1699 to 1702 Mr Dipper.

The building was rented by Mr John Lewis, the Richmond Brewer, from 1742 to 1772 and remained an ale house until 1790.

John Lewis - The Richmond Brewer - copy of a Mezzotint in Richmond Library - From a portrait by T Stewart

The Hope   22 Mortlake High Street

The Hope is another of Mortlake's old beer houses which no longer exists. The plot of land on which the building once stood has now been incorporated in the road widening of Mortlake High Street and the site is now occupied by an office block.

Hawkes & Co., had been established at Bishop Stortford in 1780 by Messrs Hawkes, Bird & Wordham with money earned from supplying malt to London Breweries via the Stort Navigation Canal. Following the purchase in 1877 by Mr James Wigan, who had previously been a partner in the Mortlake Brewery, Hawkes & Co., started selling Entire, an early name for porter and a beer that travelled well, at The Hope in 1878. They continued to do so at least until 1882, for the order book for that period shows that they sometimes took three deliveries a week!

The landlord from 1878 to 1882 was Mr Robert George Aldington, who later moved to The Express Hotel at Kew Bridge. Mr Aldington took his first delivery of Hawkes & Co., beer on 9 November 1878 which comprised one barrel of X (36 Gallons) at £1:16:0 and one Kiln of XXXX (18 Gallons) at £1:10:0, and on 23 November he obtained £0:1:0 per gallon on returned beer. By March 1879 he was taking over eleven barrels a month whilst a sign in the window during that year indicated that A1 Burton Ale was also available on draught.

During August 1880 a total of nine and three quarter barrels (351 Gallons) of beer were ordered. If this seems a large quantity of beer to have consumed in a month, one must realise that The Hope was open from 8.00 am to 11.00 pm and one can envisage the brewery workers drinking their porter under the dingy gaslights of The Hope.

Landlords:-   1882   B Edmonds   1884   Mrs Elizabeth Edmonds
               1886   Mr George Ware

The Herald, which began as an eight page paper at a penny with six columns to the page and more than seventy trade advertisements, included under the heading "Mortlake News" the transfer of the license of The Hope beer house in Mortlake High Street from Mrs Elizabeth Edmonds to Mr George Ware.

Landlord:-   1899 - 1900   Mr George Jackman

The last landlord in 1905 - 1906 was a Mr Henry Richard Butt for in 1907 Mr A Green opened the premises as Dining Rooms.

The Hope - Mortlake High Street - c 1879 - Photograph by Simpson Brothers of Cambridge

The Jolly Maltman   Mortlake High Street

There was a small linen draper's shop in the High Street kept by Mr Richard Benham. This house was owned by Mr John Biggs in 1839. It was afterwards altered and opened by Mr Matthew Lipscombe in 1843 as a beer house, under the sign of The Jolly Maltman. Mr Lipscombe afterwards went to Australia.

The Kings Arms   Thames Street

The Kings Arms was built, according to Mr J E Anderson, who used to go there for the Churchwardens' dinners, sometime in George III's reign, (1760 - 1820) although there could have been a public house there long before. The Kings Arms was an old fashioned square built house with some cobble stones in front, with steps leading up to the front door, and was the only place where post horses and chaises could be hired.

A silver pint marked at the bottom Jof Kerfhaw Mortlake was stolen from The Kings Arms at Mortlake, Surrey in 1764. "Whoever will give information to John Jenkins at The Kings Arms aforesaid, Fo that the pint may be had again shall receive Half a Guinea Reward; if offered to be pawned or fold, pray give me information as above, and you fhal receive the true reward."

From the Land Tax Records in conjunction with the Licensed Victuallers Recognizances it has been possible to trace the landlords of The Kings Arms back to the year 1780 - 1781 when Mrs Anne Phillips was the licensee. She was succeeded by Mr David Elson. In 1784 the landlord was Mr John Barker, who died the following year, and was interred in the old Churchyard. He was succeeded by his widow Sarah Barker who remained there until 1797. From 26 June 1794 and for upwards of five weeks not less than nine men and ten horses belonging to the Eleventh Regiment of the Light Dragoons were quartered and billeted at The Kings Arms, which at that time had twelve regular standings.

The owner of The Kings Arms in 1798 was a Mr Kean Fitzgerald, and in that year Mr John Taylor took over as licensee, he was followed by Mr James Price (1800 - 1801). Between 1801 and 1823 the Chiswick based brewery firm of Fuller Smith and Turner Ltd. had a leasehold interest in The Kings Arms. During this time there was a continual change of landlord namely:-

1802 - 1803	Mr Thomas Price	1804 - 1805	Mr Joseph Knapp
1806 - 1807	Mr Thomas Smith	1808 - 1810	Mrs Elizabeth Smith
1811	Mr Joseph Smith	1812 - 1816	Mr Thomas Russell
1817	Mr Robert Newton	1818 - 1821	Mr William Taylor

which suggests that even the leaseholders were having difficulty in obtaining satisfactory tenants.

The landlord in 1822 was Mr Samuel Taylor and he remained there until 1841, when Mr John Boake took over. In 1844 Boake became a director of the Richmond Conveyance Company, but stayed on as landlord until 1846. At this time the public house was known as The Kings Arms and Posting House.

The rate book of 25 November 1836 states that the owner of The Kings Arms was Mr Thomas Fitzgerald, whilst the rate book of 15 May 1863 states that the owner was Fitzgerald. The last landlord was Mr John Firmston (31 May 1855 - 1867), who was a tall wiry man. Just before

The Kings Arms was pulled down sometime between 1867 and 1871 he went to The Queens Head for a short while, and then settled down in a small beer house at the West End, on the south side of Lower Richmond Road called The Jolly Milkman, where he died on 31 May 1888, in his seventy-seventh year.

The first Odd Fellows Lodge set up in Mortlake was the Loyal Penrhyn Lodge, No 5321 Manchester Unity. It was granted its dispensation on 9 May 1865 and formed part of the Richmond District, with a membership of 26 and held its meetings at The Kings Arms Inn. The Odd Fellows Lodges in the 19th century were basically men's social clubs - as well as following their original premise to give mutual help in times of death, sickness and unemployment.

Thames Street - Mortlake - c 1770 - by S H Grimm - the trees on the right indicating the north east corner of the present green. The inn with its royal coat of arms is the Kings Arms, rebuilt and named the Mortlake Hotel - Reproduced by kind permission of the British Museum

The Lord Napier   75 Mortlake High Street

The Lord Napier for over one hundred years backed onto the river, but there the similarity with its neighbour Ye White Hart ended. For they differed in size, shape and decor. Smallness and tapestry – covered chairs and stools, gave the former a certain homely comfort.

Landlords:-			Mr Thomas Dellar
    1884			Mr George Pocock
    1886			Mrs Charlotte Pocock
    1899 - 1900		Mrs Charlotte Field
    1905			Mr Thomas Chas Alloway
    1906			Mrs Charlotte Field
    1919 - 1927		Mrs Gwendoline Tancock
    1939			Mr Thomas James Harding

The Lord Napier in the late 1940's and early 1950's had a dart board, a piano and also a bar billiards table for its patrons to occupy their leisure time.

In September 1982, Tim and Margaret Butler welcomed patrons to a superbly refurbished public house and offered a wide selection of hot and cold lunchtime food daily along with snacks available in the evening. The patrons at this time had a choice of two bars.

In October 1982, Sunday lunches were commenced with reduced rates for children. Also from October The Lord Napier were featuring a wine and cocktail bar which was open to all customers who were also offered a varied menu.

On Friday 16 August 1985 The Lord Napier was officially re-opened, by Mr G W Parson, the Managing Director of Watney, Combe, Reid, under the new management of Pat and Linda Murphy.

The Lord Napier - Mortlake High Street - Looking towards Sheen Lane

Much of the borough's bedsit population in 1985 were disappointed over the Christmas holiday, particularly on Christmas evening, to find many of the area's public houses closed. Praise was abundant for Pat and Linda Murphy of The Lord Napier, who opened their doors. "We are here to give as well as take and knew there were regular customers who were alone over Christmas," said Linda. A spokesman for Watneys Brewery said, "We are always pleased to hear of publicans who appreciate local needs."

After being closed for almost a week, Watney's riverside public house The Lord Napier re-opened for trading on Thursday 18 August 1988, under the new management of Paul and Tracey Tiernan.

In May 1996, developers applied for planning permission to change the use of the former The Lord Napier, with the intention of dividing it into office space and a nursery. Richmond Council's Planning Committee heard the case after a period of consultation.

The Lord Napier was a Victorian public house which fronted onto Mortlake High Street and backed onto the river. Having been closed for a number of years, the red brick building occupied a prime site and had been the subject of several planning applications made by housing developers in the past. An application to demolish The Lord Napier and build flats was withdrawn earlier in 1998 after Richmond Council refused Conservation Area consent.

At the Planning Sub - committee in November 1998 Michael Shanly Homes Ltd. outlined plans to make two self - contained flats and two self - contained maisonettes. A new three storey building, connecting the original building, would add a further two flats.

The Lord Napier - Mortlake High Street - 1961 - Looking west

> **NOW IT'S IN NEW HANDS, IT'S LIKE A NEW PUB.**
>
> Don't worry if you're a stranger to our pub – we're new here, too. So come along and get to know us. And become one of our very first regulars.
>
> **THE LORD NAPIER RE-OPENS FRIDAY 16th AUGUST**
>
> Enjoy a welcome from your new hosts Pat and Linda.
>
> 75 MORTLAKE HIGH STREET SW14

Under this proposal the original facade of The Lord Napier would remain intact. A council officer said, "It is considered that the proposal offers substantial benefits to the appearance and character of The Lord Napier and to this part of the Conservation Area."

The Lord Napier - Mortlake High Street - 2000 - As it is today following conversion to housing

The Mortlake Hotel   1 Mortlake High Street

The Mortlake Hotel which was built on the site of The Kings Arms, no longer exists, having closed its doors on 3 March 1955. The three-storey brick building, dating from 1866, in a semi circular style with sash windows, still stands today and was for many years Watney's staff canteen.

Landlords:-   1872 - 1873   Mr Henry Francis Huntley
               1878 - 1890   Mr Henry Collins

The Rate Book of 10 June 1891 states that Watney & Co. were the owners, and their landlord was Isabel Barker.

On 2 April 1892 Mortlake Football and Athletic Sports Club had a smoking concert at The Mortlake Hotel. A large appreciative audience enjoyed a good exhibition of skill with the bones and clog dancer. The comic element was well represented too.

Landlords:-   1895 - 1905   Mrs Isabel Webb
               1919   Mr Walter Durham
               1927   Knowland Bros

The East Sheen unit of the Volunteer Defence Corps. held a very successful dance at the York Rooms at The Mortlake Hotel in 1937. Music was provided by the Arcady Band and there were numerous novelties and spot prizes to be won. Inquires concerning the work of the Volunteer Defence Corps., which was a self supporting and voluntary organisation, were welcomed by Capt. R G Morris at 154 Upper Richmond Road East Sheen.

Landlord:-   1939   Mr Alfred Jennings

The Old George   40 Mortlake High Street

The Old George no longer exists, having finally closed its doors to the public on 1 August 1968. The building was demolished later that year to make way for the Council's High Street widening plan. It was, however, one of the oldest established public houses in Mortlake, and was situated on the south side of Mortlake High Street opposite Watney's Brewery.

The date when The George was first established is uncertain but in 1700 Mr Richard Ffitzwater, glazier, of Mortlake was admitted as proprietor of "one messuage or tenement, now four, with yard, orchard, half an acre, formally in occupation of Mr John Russet, tapestry workman, and afterwards of Susannah Holden, butting on Mortlake Street (High Street)."

In his will Mr Richard Ffitzwater left to "my loving wife Ann Ffitzwater all that my copyhold messuage or tenement, commonly known by the sign of The George in Mortlake Street with outhouses, barn and garden ground" and after her decease to his four children.

When Richard Ffitzwater died in 1703 his wife Ann was admitted to the copyhold mentioned above and it remained in the Ffitzwater family until 1745 when Mr Edward Ffitzwater "surrendered and released four messuages, formerly one messuage, formally in the occupation of Mr John Russet, Susannah Holden, then Mr John Leaver, the widow Brushwood,--------- - Bagnall and Francis Heal, now to Mr Thomas Stove."

In 1773 Sarah Saunders, wife of Mr William Saunders, potter, was admitted as proprietor. The landlord between 1780 and 1789 was a Mr William Jacobs and when he died he was succeeded by his widow Mrs Elizabeth Jacobs, who remained in tenure until 1791. In 1789 John Saunders, potter, and his wife Mary were admitted as customary tenants, however in 1792 they surrendered "all that customary messuage or tenement called or known by the sign of The George, late in the tenure of Mrs Elizabeth Jacobs and then of John Wyatt, victualler" to Mr

The Old George - Mortlake High Street - c 1893 - Interior - From a drawing by Albert Betts

John Edward Waring of Barnes, who was duly admitted.

Sometime during 1791 Mr John Wyatt, victualler, took over as landlord and stayed until 1803. From 26 June 1794 and for upwards of five weeks not less than seven men and six horses belonging to the Eleventh Regiment of Light Dragoons were quartered and billeted at The George, which at that time had no stabling for the horses.

In 1803, Mr James Cox became the landlord and continued until 1826 when Mr Samuel Cox took over. Up and until this time it was simply The George, the adjective "Old" being in use by 1826. Perhaps it was out of respect for the memory of the popular King George III, who had died in 1820.

The rate book of 25 November 1836 states that the owner of The Old George is Young and Bainbridge and their landlord at that time was Mr George Day, he was succeeded by his wife in 1855 and she continued as landlady until 1862.
Landlords:-

1863 - 1867	Mr William Martin	1871	Mr John Eagles
1872	Mr George Englefield	1876	S Allsorp
1878 - 1884	Mr Rowland Alfred Davies	1890	Mr George Orchin

The Old George - Mortlake High Street - c 1912/34

The Old George - Mortlake High Street - c 1960 - south side looking west - brewery frontage north side

The rate book of 10 June 1891 states that the owner of The Old George is Young & Co.

Landlords:-

November	1893	Mr Edward Cox
July	1904	W J Hall
1 December	1911	S Aldridge
21 November	1912	Mr Hubert Owen Barrett
24 October	1934	E J T Hodge
23 July	1935	W J Coleman
22 December	1936	Mr Richard Joseph Penketh (paid £1000 to predecessor all at.)

On Contract of 3 December 1936 is a memo:- The purchaser fully understands that there is a road or housing scheme on foot which may effect the property and he is prepared to accept any risk which may be involved.

The Old George was always a social centre, the Odd Fellows held their meetings here, as did the James Wigan Lodge 635 of the Ancient Order of Druids in 1937.

On 11 May 1942 Mr Thomas Price became the landlord and when he died on 4 September 1947 his widow Mrs Gwendolyn Barbara Price continued as landlady. She was succeeded on 30 September 1952 by Mr Arthur Edward Victor Harwood and he was succeeded on 11 October 1960 by the last landlord Mr Walter Edward Clegg, who died on 30 June 1968.

During the 1950's The Old George had a dart board in one of its bars where the patrons could entertain themselves for a few hours each day. Inside the ceilings were very low and the floors were uneven and at varying levels. At the back was the Old George Assembly Rooms for receptions and dances with stables next door. The opening at the side was a patent brick alley known as Old George Passage, which often had a lot of empties stacked up awaiting collection by the Ram Brewery of Young & Co. and there was always a strong odour of ale there. The passage had gates which were closed once a year and the entrance to the public house was half way down this passage.

The site of The Charlie Butler alongside The Old George - Mortlake High Street - 1968

The Queens Head   Mortlake Waterfront

The Queens Head is another of Mortlake's old established public houses which no longer exists. The building, which still stands overlooking the river Thames, was converted into flats as Tapestry Court when the license was transferred to The Lord Napier in 1952. There were two routes that patrons could take to reach this public house, one was by way of Tapestry Alley, the other was along the towpath.

The Queens Head was built early in the eighteenth century by Philip Bourne on land purchased after the closure of the Tapestry Works. The first landlord of whom we have a record is Mr Henry Elcock in 1780, who may possibly have held the freehold as well since after his death in 1787 his wife Mrs Susannah Elcock continued as landlady until 1799. From 26 June 1794 and for upwards of five weeks not less than eight men and seven horses belonging to the Eleventh Regiment of Light Dragoons were quartered and billeted at The Queens Head, which at that time had ten regular standings. The freehold then came into the possession of Mrs Mary Davis from 1799 until her death in 1822 and during that time there were six landlords, namely;-

1800 - 1803	Mr William Butcher	1804 - 1805	Mr Samuel Lund
1806	Mr William Clark	1807 - 1811	Mr William Wood
1813 - 1818	Mr Henry Carmen	1819 - 1824	Mr George Langridge

On Friday 22 August 1823 at twelve o'clock the freehold and copyhold houses and tenements of the late Mrs Mary Davis, comprising The Queens Head and a neat dwelling house on the bank of the Thames, three brick built tenements in Queen's Head Court and four copyhold tenements with a plot of ground in the several occupations of Mr Langridge, Miss Edmonds, Mrs Sims, the widow Benham and others were to be sold by auction by Mr Squibb and Son at Garraway's Coffee House, Chance Alley, Cornhill, in four lots.

The particulars of lot one were:-

A valuable freehold estate, comprising The Queens Head public house, in the occupation of Mr Langridge, pleasantly situated at the bottom end of Queen's Head Court, facing the Thames, containing on the ground floor a Taproom. A Bar and Parlour, a Tea Drinking room looking to the river, a small Tea Drinking room under the Clubroom, with Kitchen, Wash - house. A large and pleasant clubroom on the First Floor with several Bedrooms and good cellaring under the buildings on the West side of the Court. Also a tenement adjoining, in the occupation of Mr John Hoare, containing four rooms.

Queens Head and Tapestry House (then derelict) - c 1868/76 - From a coloured lithograph by Albert Betts

The Queens Head - Mortlake - c 1879 - when it was a Hawkes & Co Inn, next door is the Hawkes & Co depot - they were brewers from Bishop Stortford Herts est 1780 - Photograph by Simpson Brothers of Cambridge

The Queens Head was let on lease for twenty-one years from October 1804 at £31: 10: 0 clear of Land Tax & C.

The tenement in the occupation of Mr John Hoare, at 3s per week = £7: 16: 0 per year, Land Tax, 6: 0 a year.

The tenant of Lot One is to have the custody of the Title Deeds, upon entering into covenants with the Purchaser of Lot Two to produce them when required.

End of particulars of lot one.

The Queens Head was bought by Susanna Mary Edwards at the auction and on 19 October 1824 Mary Nalton is recorded as being the landlady. The Mortlake Independent Friendly Society was set up in Mortlake in 1824 and they held their meetings at The Queens Head. The Society was basically a men's social club that existed to give mutual help in times of hardship.

In the following year Mr John Biggs of Barnes was recorded as being the owner (1825 - 1837), and on 17 October 1826 his landlord was a Mr William Tew who remained there until 1839. The Rate Book of 31 October 1839 records a Mr Scott as the landlord and he was succeeded by his widow Mrs Mary Scott in 1843. The Rate Book of 21 October 1846 records a Mr William Davies as the landlord and he was succeeded by his widow Mrs Betsy Davies.

The most notable landlord, however, was almost certainly Francis Richard Godfrey, who came in 1862. A waterman to Her Majesty the Queen, during his period, The Queens Head became a famous meeting place for the boating fraternity and Anderson records:

"Godfrey held regattas and I recollect going to one of them, when I saw him in his waterman's uniform get into a large tub with a number of geese attached to tow him along. The poor geese fluttered about with the ribbons round their necks and got into inextricable confusion and one had to be killed through getting nearly strangled. It ended, I recollect, in a regular fiasco. Of course there was the usual cannon firing from a cellar flap about four or five feet from the towpath. On one occasion a man, known as 'Simmy', was nearly killed passing at the time the cannon was fired; as it was a small portion of his nose was blown away."

Godfrey died on 1 May 1868 and was buried in Mortlake cemetery. He was followed at The Queens Head by Mr John Firmston (1868 - 1876), a tall, wiry man, who had been the last landlord of The King's Arms, probably leaving about the time when the second auction took place on 11 August 1876.

The sale particulars give no reason for the sale but show that the estate covered the same properties as in 1823 except for the four copyhold cottages in the High Street. Lot one covered The Queens Head itself, and was described in the most glowing terms as:

"The well - known and far famed old Boating House .... A most important situation, and one possessing association of interest to all boating men, and commanding the eager attention of the public on all aquatic occasions of interest, being within a few hundred yards of the winning post on the recognised rowing course from Putney to Mortlake. The house contains numerous Bed Rooms, Club Room, Tea Room; and in addition to all necessary internal adjuncts for Trade purposes, possesses outside accommodation for large numbers of Guests and Spectators. It is let to Messrs Phillips, Wigan & Co, the Brewers, of Mortlake, on an Annual Tenancy, at the Rental of £40 per annum."

Sometime during August 1877 the inquest into the murder of Patrick Hurley, a market garden labourer, who had been found among the gooseberry bushes in the Lower Richmond Road, was held at The Queens Head.

The landlord between 1879 and 1882 was Mr Henry Charles Fuhr, and in the early 1880's advertised in the window that he sold Hawkes & Co's Pale Ale. Other landlords were 1884 Mr William Huntsman, 1886 Martimus R Chambers, and 1890 Eleazor M Butler.

The Rate Book of 10 June 1891 records that the owner and occupier are Watney & Co., and is probably the time when Philip Bourne's House was demolished and replaced with a larger but much less attractive three - storey building which continued as The Queens Head until, after almost two hundred and fifty years, it closed in 1952.

Landlords:-
- 1895 -   Mr Anton Carl Heinrick Gustave Deitrich
- 1899 -   Mr Leonard Budd
- 1905 - 1906   Mr Walter George White
- 1916 - 1919   Mr William Peter Fitchett
- 1927 - 1928   Mr Percy F Roberts

The last landlords were John Kelly, who came in 1937, and his wife, who ran the house after the 1939 - 43 War assisted by her eldest daughter Grace, the third wife to succeed her husband at The Queens Head. After the Queens Head closed, Mrs Kelly moved only a short distance down river to The Lord Napier.

The Queens Head in its later years had four bars on the ground floor, one of which had a dart board. Upstairs, however, was a very large room where there was a further dart board, two full-sized snooker tables and a table tennis table.

The Three Tuns   Lower Richmond Road

In 1740 The Three Tuns was occupied by Mr Christopher Flinn, victualler. It was sometime during the year 1745 under the will of Mr Adam Ffunnel, butcher, of Mortlake that Mary Brinkworth was admitted to "All that messuage with outhouses, yard and garden in Mortlake called or known by the sign of The Three Tuns."

Exactly when The Three Tuns changed its name to The Jolly Gardeners is not clear for the Wimbledon Court Rolls mention both names in 1796, however, in 1798 the reference clearly states that The Three Tuns, now known as The Jolly Gardeners, was formerly in occupation of Mr Thomas Cawdry, then Mr Christopher Flinn, then Edwards and late Mr John Mander.

Lower Richmond Road - Mortlake - c 1770 - by S H Grimm - the inn on the left at the junction of Ship Lane is the old Three Tuns, now rebuilt and named the Jolly Gardeners - Reproduced by kind permission of the British Museum

The Two Brewers   52 Mortlake High Street

One of the oldest public houses, The Two Brewers, is another of Mortlake's public houses that no longer exists having closed its doors for the last time on Thursday night 20 October 1961. The building was situated on the south side of Mortlake High Street only a few doors away from The Old George.

It is not known when the inn was first established but the Licensed Victuallers Recognizances show that in 1786 a Mr Peter Moff was the landlord. From 26 June 1794 and for upwards of five weeks not less than six men and six horses belonging to the Eleventh Regiment of Light Dragoons were quartered and billeted at The Two Brewers, which at that time had no stabling for the horses. When Mr Peter Moff died in 1797 his widow Mrs Sarah Moff took over as landlady and remained in occupation until 1818.

"Leaves from an old Ledger"

"Mrs Moff - The Two Brewers" (1806) - Reference in the introduction of these notices was made to the large supplies delivered to The Two Brewers which was evidently a favourite house of call for lightermen and others engaged on the river. Before the introduction of railways the waterways were the chief means of transit for merchandise. It may be that the bargees preferred the Mortlake Brew to any other, and provisioned themselves for their journeys to Reading or Oxford.

taken from The Herald 12 August 1922.

The property belonged between 1786 - 1788 to a Eddie Land and in 1789 it passed to Wallingers who held it until 1803. In the following year Messrs Halford & Co. Ltd. became the

The Two Brewers - Mortlake High Street

owners and their landlord from 1819 - 1827 was Mr Thomas Souster, 1828 Mr Edward Prince, 1829 - 1835 Mr Thornton. Between 1836 - 1854 Messrs Edn Weatherstone & Co. Ltd. were the owners and their landlord was Mr George Thornton 1836 - 1846, to be followed by Mr Thomas M Thornton.

The Royal Victoria Benefit Society was set up in Mortlake in 1854 and they held their meetings at The Two Brewers. At what time during the day and at what frequency the Benefit Society meetings were held is unknown. The Society was basically a men's social club.

In 1855 the property belonged to the local brewers Phillips and Wigan and their landlords were 1855 - 1862 Mr John Squire, 1863 - 1875 Mr William Sumner, and 1875 - 1882 Mr Henry Jellett. The licence issued to Mr Henry Jellett on 1 March 1875 described "The Two Brewers as a type "A" ale house." What this means has yet to be discovered.

The Two Brewers - Mortlake High Street

In 1882 the property passed to Phillips & Co and their landlords were 1882 - 1887 Mr Charles Joseph Churchill, 1887 - 1888 Mr George Thomas Fairall, Theresa Fairall, 1889 - 1890 Jonadab Hanks. Sometime during 1889 Phillips & Co were taken over by Watney & Co. who became the new owners and their landlords were 1890 - 1895 Mr Peter Matthew Ward and 1895 - 1926 Mr Frederick Pugh. With the amalgamation of Combe, Reid and Watney & Co. during 1902 and the formation of a new company Watney, Combe, Reid Co. Ltd. in 1903, The Two Brewers had another new owner. During the final three years of its life the house came under the ownership of Watney Mann Ltd.

The remaining landlords were 1926 - 1941 Mr Ernest Edward Wederall, 1941 - 1950 Mr William James Frederick Pugh, 1950 Mr Alexander Frederick Bishop, 1950 - 1953 Mr Frank Brown, 1953 - 1958 Mr Charles Frederick Henden, 1958 Mrs Jessie Maud Henden, 1958 Mr Kenneth Leslie Balls, and finally 1959 - 1961 Mr John Canen Gamsey.

The Whitworth Arms   93 Mortlake High Street

The Whitworth Arms is another of Mortlake's old beer houses which no longer exists, and appears to have been no more than a small beer house, the earliest reference found is in the 1881 Census.

Landlord:-   1900   Mr Thomas Potter
              1902 – 1903   Mr George Jesse Jones

The Blue Anchor   Site Unknown

John Bourn, was the local waterman, with boats for the transport of people and merchandise to London and elsewhere. When John moved to The Blue Anchor in 1601 or 1602, his son Henry, and daughter-in-law took over the Church House and the waterman business. (see also The Maidenhead)

In the early years of the 17th century there lived at Mortlake in a house by the river, at the west end of the High Street, Augustine Phillips, Shakespearean actor and a favourite comedian. He was one of The Lord Chamberlain's Company of Players of which the members were called "Fellows". They were a happy group bursting with good humour and fellowship and apparently free from the rancour which so often disturbs artistic circles. It was only eleven and a quarter miles by river from Southwark to the Mortlake landing place, and one of Henry Bourn's boats was roomy enough to convey the players and their luggage from the Globe at Southwark to Mortlake, where the Company would settle down to discuss future plans, rehearse old plays and try out others that anyone pulled out of the bag. In their off - hours they would visit John Bourn's Blue Anchor to assuage their thirst.

In 1617 Symon Willes held the copyhold of "one messuage anciently called the Hartshornes, now the Blew Anckor, with barne, orchard and yarde, lyeinge south of the Ryver of Thames, north of William Basse, east of the Church land, west of the highwaye from the watersyde to Mortelake town".

This could possibly be the forerunner of the present Ship Inn, we know that a house for the purveyance of refreshment to thirsty travellers has existed in this vicinity for over four hundred years.

The Hart's Horn   Site Unknown

A tavern of sorts has been situated on the south bank of the Thames in the vicinity of Ship Lane since the sixteenth century. In Shakespearian times the public house was called The Hart's Horn, and would have been the regular drinking place of the bargees bringing hops and malt to the old London Brewery which stood next door.

The Hornes   Site Unknown

'From the Survey of Mortlake in 1617'

After an orchard with a piece of land and a stable, was "one house anciently called 'The Hornes', with a cottage, orchard and garden adjoining," the property of Thomas Fletcher. The inn must have been in the hands of Fletcher or his father for many years. In the Parish Accounts for 1584, when one of the church bells had to be recast, is a payment of one shilling, "For two of the bell founders dinners at Fletchers." This could possibly be the site of The Old George.

The Maidenhead   Site Unknown

'From the Survey of Mortlake in 1617'

Beyond the footway still stands the "Church House with barne and an outhouse," probably built in the sixteenth century and given to the parish for the upkeep of the church and the comfort of the poor. At the time of the survey it was occupied by Henry Bourn, the local waterman and one of the survey "jurors". On the nearby shingle his boats lay beached at the ebb, and at the flood they thumpity-thumped against the mooring post. Henry's house was sometimes called The Maidenhead.

In 1636, in a small book *Taverns in the Ten Shires Round London* published by John Taylor (the water poet), he mentions that The Maidenhead was kept by Phoebe Tucker.

The Maidenhead in 1745 was situated somewhere on the bank of the river in the vicinity of The Ship, when it was described as "All that messuage or tenement or inn, commonly called The Maidenhead, with gardens, orchard, backsides, outhouses and appurtenances."

Inn Signs Past and Present

The study of inn signs and inn names can be most revealing, both in dating inns and in giving some hints about their pasts; however it can also be thoroughly misleading.

Inn names had their period of vogue, and some of them can be definitely associated with some individual, family, or trade. Often an inn took its name from the feudal landlord; for instance, a Bear & Ragged Staff will have formed part of the estates of the Earls of Warwick, the White lion, of the Howard Dukes of Norfolk, and the Blue Boar, of the Earls of Oxford, these symbols being part of their coats of arms.

The earliest ale house sign was, as is commonly known, a branch of greenery tied to a pole, and known as the bush or ale stake. This custom dates back to the Romans, who used a vine branch for the same purpose. There are today many public houses called the Bush, or Hop Pole, which was the same thing but in early days they would have had no names and would have been known by the name of the owner. The first inn names as we know them came in the twelfth century, when monks began to build hospices on a large scale for pilgrims.

The advantage of erecting a hanging sign rather than merely painting on the walls was that it could be seen by potential customers at a distance, and in a village where there were several ale houses, the landlords would compete for the largest, gaudiest and most attractive sign - mediaeval neon, in effect. In 1375 an act had to be passed limiting the ale stake's projection over the roadway to seven feet and in time the inn sign had become so universal that the uprooting of a sign by the authorities signified the suppression of the inn.

In Charles I's time these signs had to have a clearance of a least nine feet to allow horsemen safe passage; after the great fire of London in 1666 a vain attempt was made to ban them altogether. During the great rebuilding that followed the fire many craftsmen involved in the work carved signs in their spare time to make a little extra cash; a now featureless wooden panel preserved in the Cock & Bottle, Fleet Street, is said to have been carved by Grinling Gibbons himself, but was more probably the work of his employees. The presence of so many of these skilled men, led to a great increase in both the quantity and extravagance of these signs, which were necessary because there was no system of street numbering. But they could be confusing. When premises changed hands they often retained their old name - hence The Rainbow coffee house in Fleet Street, founded in 1657, occupied a former dyer's shop. Or it might keep its old sign and be given a new one too - one can only imagine what might have been sold at The Civet Cat and Three Herrings.

Addison, writing in The Spectator in 1710, commented: "I have seen the Goat set up before a perfumer's and a King's head before a swordcutler's." In time it reached the point where the sign alone would not tell the customer whether the premises was a goldsmith's or a brothel; and although the hundreds of gaily painted signboards swinging overhead must have made a very colourful street scene, there was a constant danger of one of them falling and causing a nasty injury. Finally in 1762 all hanging signs, except those belonging to taverns and pawnshops, were banned from the City of London, in 1764 from Westminster and in 1768 the street - numbering system we know today was instituted.

Present Day Inn Signs - Barnes

The Bridge	Bridges feature in many public house names. The sign at Barnes depicts the second Hammersmith Bridge designed by Sir J Bazalgette, Chief Engineer to the Metropolitan Board of Works.
Coach and Horses	A common public house name in all parts of Britain since the seventeenth century. There are more than fifty in the London Area. Often denoted a change house for the coach, and post chaise horses. The arrival of Hackney carriages, forerunners of modern taxis and later the introduction of stage - coaches meant that there was plenty of traffic on the roads. Inns were natural stopping places, providing refreshments for both horses and humans.
Halfway House	These public houses were originally on country roads and indicated convenient stopping places for travellers.
Rose of Denmark	A reference to Alexandra, Princess of Wales, who was Danish by birth. The wild rose was her favourite flower, and as Queen Alexandra she inaugurated Alexandra Rose day in 1912 to mark her fiftieth year of residence in England. Rose emblems were sold to the public to raise money for hospitals, a practice which still continues today.
The Sun	The early use of the Sun as a tavern sign made use of its simple visual form. It was painted as a circle with a few rays around it.
The White Hart	The earliest instance of this very common sign coincides with the beginning of Richard II's reign in 1377, and it was that monarch's heraldic symbol. It had the advantage in any case of being a highly distinctive visual symbol at a time when the hart, the male deer, was possibly more familiar to the average person than it is today. The continued use of the White Hart in later centuries is explained by its having become a generic term for a tavern.

Present Day Inn Signs – East Sheen

Hare and Hounds   Always a popular sign with many variations.

Pig and Whistle   This name is neither as common as is normally supposed, nor is it very old. When Lilleywhite examined 17,000 London signs up to the nineteenth century he was unable to find a single example of Pig and Whistle. Would seem straight forwardly rural if it were not for the inexplicable presence of the whistle. A theory has been advanced that the phrase is a corruption of the Danish "Pige – washail" – here's health to the girls; but the pig might be related to the Saxon "piggin", a pail, surviving from days when ale was served in buckets and customers dipped their own mugs, or pigs into it.

The Plough   This remains one of the commonest public house names in Britain, having been in regular use since the sixteenth century. A sign that is to be found in every agricultural district, for Plough Monday, the first Monday after the twelve days of the Christmas festivities, was a very special occasion – the beginning of a new agricultural year. Decorated ploughs would be dragged in procession to raise "Plough money" for an ale frolic. On these occasions gentlemen feasted their farmers and they in turn their men.

Present Day Inn Signs – Mortlake

Charlie Butler   Derives its name from the man who worked as head horse keeper at Young & Co Brewery for forty three years.

Jolly Gardeners   Commemorates a past local industry.

Jolly Milkman   Thought to be the only one in the country.

Railway Tavern   The coming of the railway in the nineteenth century made a huge impact on life in Britain and this was naturally reflected in the naming of public houses.

The Ship   A common sign, especially close to water.

Past Inn Signs - Barnes

The Boileau	At one time the inn sign depicted the arms of Boileau de Castelnau.
The Edinburgh Castle	At one time the sign that hung outside this public house depicted the the castle at Edinburgh.
The Market Gardener	The inn sign at one time depicted a local market gardener by the name of John or Johnny Biggs as he was called, wearing a tall black hat, sitting on his black horse and holding a glass of ale in his right hand.
The Red Rover	Named after one of the stage coaches which regularly ran from London to Southampton.

Past Inn Signs - East Sheen

The Bull	A very popular name and sign. In the earliest days this was a religious sign derived from La Boule (Latin Bulla) the seal put on a document or letter of a collegiate body or monastery. Later the bull became popular all over the British Isles due largely to the horrible bull baiting so popular in Tudor and Stuart England and not in fact prohibited by law until 1835. The animal was tethered to an iron ring set in the ground and specially trained dogs were set upon it. It is also used in heraldry, the arms of Richard Duke of York, and the house of York and many others.
The Derby Arms	The sign depicted one of the Derby races held on Epsom Downs.
The Victoria	England's longest reigning sovereign born 1819, daughter of the Duke of Kent. She was, for a time, the most popular monarch. A very common sign which shows loyalty to the throne and sympathy.

Past Inn Signs - Mortlake

Lord Napier	The sign showed a portrait of Lord Napier.
Pickled Newt	The sign showed a newt.
Queens Arms	The sign at one time showed a coat of arms; and latterly showed a waving arm.
The Spur	The sign depicted a train crossing a set of points; indicating that it was taking a different route.

Present Day Inn Signs – Barnes

Present Day Inn Signs - Barnes

Present Day Inn Signs - East Sheen

Present Day Inn Signs - Mortlake

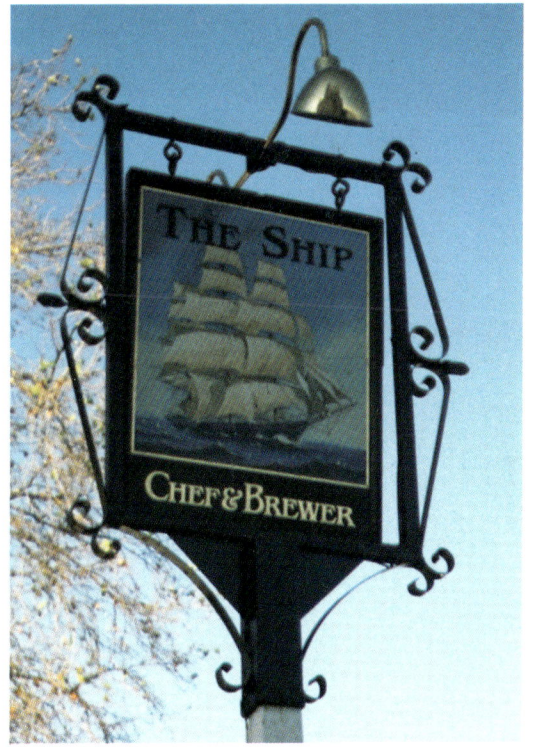

Present Day Inn Signs – Mortlake

Past Inn Signs - Barnes

Past Inn Signs - East Sheen

Past Inn Signs - Mortlake

Tokens

In contrast to a coin, which is a piece of metal of a certain value, issued by Government to circulate as legal tender, a token is privately struck without Royal or Parliamentary approval. However, since they are used in the same manner as coins, the public generally accepts them as a form of money, even though they may only be redeemed for goods.

During the middle ages, silver was very scarce, and prices were very low. The silver penny was about the size of a silver three - penny piece, therefore, it was valuable, but too large in value for the low price of goods. In 1330 it was pointed out that as beer was one penny for three gallons, and the penny being the smallest coin, therefore, a great demand was made for a smaller valued coin, hence the birth of the token.

The want of authorised money for small change had begun to make itself felt as far back as the reign of Elizabeth I (1558 - 1603). The Government had coined one penny, halfpence and farthing pieces in silver, but the latter were necessarily so small and thin as to be a loss rather than a gain to the trader. German copper coins were then imported and used, some known as abbey-pieces and others as Nuremburg counters; for Elizabeth I had a magnificent contempt for any other than the precious metal to bear her authorised effigy.

James I (1603 - 1625) made some attempt to deal with the shortage of small change. He delegated his prerogative of striking copper money to Lord Harrington, (sic, actually Harington) who was given a patent for striking farthings. It was, with all due benevolence, stated that such pieces were to relieve the lot of "the people who, in the days when a penny was a lot of money, were suffering by reason of there being no smaller value coin with which to make minor purchases."

Similar patents were issued in the next reign, but the privilege was grossly abused by the patentees, and their refusal to re-change these farthings caused so great a loss to tradesmen, that in consequence of public demand, the coins were suppressed by Parliament in 1664. An authorised official minor currency was intended, but it was never brought into use owing to the Civil War. Tokens immediately began to be issued in 1649 by towns, tradesmen and occasionally by private persons, without authority, but as stated on some tokens "for necessarie chainge." During the whole of the Commonwealth no copper coinage was officially issued, and tokens continued to be the small currency of the country till regal copper coinage was started under Charles II in 1672. The Royal Proclamation announcing the new currency forbade the use of all others. (i.e. Tokens).

Thus there came into being, between 1649 and about 1672, a series known to collectors as "Seventeenth Century Tokens." Since they were almost officially accepted, were purely local issues, were struck in large quantities and reasonably inexpensive, they are an interesting series for any local historian.

This series of Seventeenth Century Tokens is catalogued in the standard reference work Boyne W., *Trade Tokens issued in the Seventeenth Century* (edited by G. C. Williamson) reprinted by B. A. Seaby, Ltd. The main issues are catalogued by county with the towns or villages within the county placed in alphabetical order. The tokens were issued by people - the man in the street - for the people, and the various issuers put their trade or occupation on their token coins. They also put their name on the obverse. Thus these little tokens open for us a window through which we may look into the past and see something of the many trades and occupations of the time.

As stated above, under the County heading of Surrey we find listed the tokens which were issued by the traders in Barnes and Mortlake.

In Barnes.

Charles Goodwin issued his tokens inscribed on the obverse 'Charles Goodwin - his Half Penny' and on the reverse 'of Barnes Vintner' - around the figure of a bear.

Thomas Emmerton, Churchwarden of Barnes, and a local vintner – 1657, issued his tokens inscribed on the obverse 'At the Blacksmith Arms' and on the reverse 'In Barnes 1667 TME.'

The Shovel at Barnes

Iames Edwards issued his farthing tokens inscribed on the obverse with the issuers name 'IAMES EDWARDS' around a malt shovel. The legend continues, on the reverse, to say 'AT BARNS 1660' around the man-and-wife triad of initials E over IA.

The Horse in Barnes

The putative 1667 Barnes halfpenny tokens listed as Surrey 6 and 7 by Williamson - one Timothy Hartley with man on horseback, the other Timothy Marley with man on horseback. Are these really one and the same? Has the diesinker in error punched M instead of H?

In Mortlake

The Merchant Taylor Arms

William Thorneton issued his tokens inscribed on the obverse 'The Merchant Taylor Arms' and on the reverse 'In Mortlake 1665 - his Half Penny'.

City Arms / The Garter

Peter White issued his halfpenny tokens inscribed on the obverse with the issuers name' Peter d White in Morteclake' around the man-and-wife triad of initials W over PD. The legend continues on the reverse to say 'Honi-Soit-Qui-Mal-y-Pense' which is the motto of The Order of the Garter around the Arms of the City of London.

These trade tokens as they were called, became legal currency as 'promises to pay', and the circulation of them in all parts of the country grew to enormous proportions. Those of the better class innkeepers were generally brass farthings, and always bore the sign of the inn from which they emanated and at which they were redeemable in the current coin of the realm.

For the convenience of re-changing the numerous varieties of tokens, tradesmen kept boxes with several divisions, into which those of the various tradesmen and corporations were sorted, and when sufficient numbers were collected, they were returned to the issuer and changed into silver or notes.

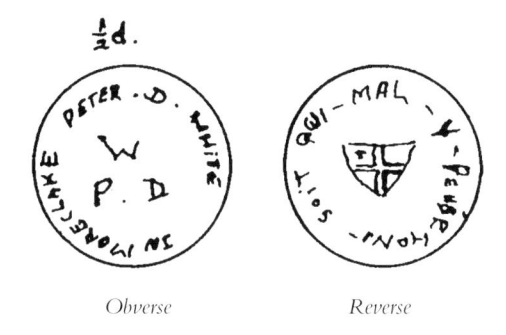

Obverse *Reverse*

Glossary

ALE HOUSE	A house selling ale and beer for consumption on, and perhaps off, the premises. Food was also usually sold.
ALE HOUSE KEEPER	A person in charge of an ale house.
ALE - SILVER	A fee or gift paid to the Lord Mayor of London for the privilege of selling ale in London.
ADMISSION	The grant by the Lord of the Manor of the right of a new owner to hold copyhold land.
ANCIENTLY	Formerly, not ancient in sense of old.
APPURTENANCE	That which belongs to something else.
BAR	The counter at which the drinks are sold, or a licensed room containing a counter.
BEDE - ALE	A drinking party at which money was raised for someone fallen on hard times.
BEER SHOP / HOUSE	A house with a licence to sell beer, but not wine or spirits. Between 1830 and 1869 such houses did not need a licence from the magistrates' court, merely one issued by the local excise office.
BEER RETAILER	The licensee of a beer shop.
BREWER	A person who brewed ale for sale by retail and also to ale houses and inns.
BREWSTER SESSIONS	Annual sessions of the licensing justices, at which licences to trade in alcoholic liquors are issued.
BRIDE - ALE	On her wedding day the bride's parents provided ale for which the guests paid.
CHURCH - ALE	A feast to commemorate the dedication of a church at which ale was sold in aid of funds for church expenses.

COPYHOLD	Land held at the will of the Lord of the Manor, originally by virtue of rendering service, but latterly by money payment; admission to the tenure of the land was entered in the Manorial Court Roll and a "copy" of the entry was given to the new owner as his title deed.
ENFRANCHISEMENT	The freeing of copyhold land by the Lord of the Manor. i.e. converting to freehold.
FREE HOUSE	A public house not owned (or tied) to a brewery. May be owned by the landlord or may be part of a chain owned by a private company who install managers. The freehold may be owned by an institution or a large estate who lease to a tenant.
HEREDITAMENT	Property inheritance.
INN	The inn in all its various meanings includes the idea of lodging - be it for students, private people using their own inn, or for travellers. The main purpose of the public or common inn was to provide lodgings and refreshment for its guests. It is likely that the idea of inns providing food and drink was not yet a generally accepted practice during the Middle Ages. This was the business of the other establishments - taverns, ale houses and other victualling houses. Tudor and Stuart inns sometimes included a tavern, a separate room selling wine to all comers, rather like a public bar in a modern hotel. In the sixteenth and seventeenth centuries, and more so in later periods, the word was sometimes carelessly used to include ale houses. On the other hand eighteenth and early nineteenth century trade directories frequently differentiated between inns, hotels, and public houses. Today the word still retains its original meaning of a place with lodgings for travellers, but it is also used to mean an old public house, particularly one in a country village or town centre.
INN HOLDER / INNKEEPER	A person in charge of an inn.
LANDLORD	The master of an inn.
LICENSEE	The person in whose name the licence is held, possibly a tenant or a manager but not necessarily either.

LICENCE STRIP	A strip above the entrance bearing the licensee's name and the extent of the licence.
MANAGED HOUSE	A house run by a manager.
MANOR	Originally a mediaeval feudal estate belonging to a nobleman with the administration of the land regulated by Manorial Courts: by the eighteenth century the courts largely survived as a means of electing village constables and for the transfer of copyhold property.
MESSUAGE	A dwelling - house and the adjoining land and buildings belonging to it.
OBVERSE	The portrait side of a coin, in the absence of a portrait the titles, legends or motifs common to the series. Often called "Heads."
OCCUPATION	Employment, calling, pursuit.
OCCUPIER	Person in (especially temporary or subordinate) possession of house etc.
POST HOUSE	An inn or other house where horses were kept ready for royal courtiers (1511 - 1635) and where post boys and post horses were kept ready to dispatch the mail to the next post house and to take and guide travellers at a rapid pace. During the coaching era the term came to mean a high class inn which provided post horses and post chaise for hire.
POSTMASTER	The innkeeper or other who ran the post office. The term was also used in the nineteenth century for the innkeeper or other who hired out post chaise and post horses.
POST BOY	1 The inn servant (or employee of the postmaster) who carried the mail. 2 The inn servant who rode with the post horses and post chaise and acted as guide.
PROPRIETOR	Holder of property; owner especially of business.

PUBLIC HOUSE	A house licensed to sell ale, beer and spirits and maybe also wine. The term first came into use in the late seventeenth century, partly as an alternative term for ale house, being a contraction of the term 'public ale house.' However, the term was not exclusively used for ale houses, but could include small inns and taverns.
REVERSE	The opposite side to the obverse of a coin, often called "Tails."
SCOT - ALE	A dinner given to tenants when they paid their rents.
SNUG	A small compartment or room not necessarily adjacent to the main bar.
TAPROOM	The common drinking room of a public house from which the public bar has since evolved.
TAVERN	The term would appear to be restricted to houses selling wine during the Middle Ages and Tudor and Stuart periods. Food was often sold at the tavern. Samuel Johnson defined a tavern as a house specialising in the sale of wine, but by the late eighteenth century there were few such taverns outside London, and the term had fallen out of use as a description of a wine house, it had come to be an alternative word for public house, a house that sold beer, spirits and wine.
TAVERNER	A person in charge of a tavern.
TENEMENT	The property held by a tenant, often synonymous with messuage.
TENURE	Condition, form of right or title, under which especially real property is held; period of holding (during his tenure of office).
TIED HOUSE	Usually owned by a brewery company, but sometimes leased by an institution or private individual to a brewery company. A house tied by trading agreement with a particular brewer.
VINTNER	A wine merchant.

References

SECTION 1
MANUSCRIPT SOURCES, DIRECTORIES, NEWSPAPERS etc

Althorp
Wimbledon Court Rolls

City of Westminster Archives Centre
Phillips More & Co. Ltd - Register of changes in publicans - 1873 - 89.
Watney & Co. Ltd. - Register of freeholds and leaseholds - 1866.
Watney Coombe Reid & Co. Ltd. - Register of changes in publicans - 1910 - 11.

Greater London Record Office
Information Leaflet No 3 - Middlesex Licensed Victuallers Records (with a note on Surrey and Kent).

Guildhall Library
Post Office London Directory Suburban South - 1900, 1902 and 1903.
Lilleywhite Collection.

Public Record Office
Innkeeper's Petitions of 1759 - 1809

Richmond Local Studies Library
Post Office London Suburban Directories.
Post Office Directory of Home Counties.
Census Returns for Barnes - 1851, 1861, 1871, 1881 and 1891.
Census Returns for Mortlake - 1851, 1861, 1871, 1881 and 1891.

Surrey Record Office
Seventeenth Century Barnes Parish Registers.
Seventeenth Century Barnes Churchwardens' Accounts.
Licensed Victualler Recognizances - 1785 - 1827, for the Parish of Barnes.
Seventeenth Century Mortlake Parish Registers.
Seventeenth Century Mortlake Churchwardens' Accounts.
Licensed Victualler Recognizances - 1785 - 1827, for the Parish of Mortlake.

SECTION 2
PUBLISHED BOOKS AND ARTICLES

Barnes and Mortlake History Society, publications
    1977 *Barnes and Mortlake as it Was.* Hendon Publishing
    1979 *Vintage Barnes and Mortlake.* Hendon Publishing
    1994 *Halfpenny Green.* Picton Publishing (Chippenham) Limited

Anderson J E   *Mortlake Memories.*
    1898 *Sheen House Mortlake and Its Inhabitants.*
    1909 *Rambles Through Mortlake.*
    1886 *A history of the Parish of Mortlake.*

Arnold P   1988 *The Complete Book of Indoor Games.* The Hamlyn Publishing Group Ltd

Ashley M   1967 *Life in Stuart England.*

Burke J   1981 *The English Inn.* B. T. Batsford Ltd

Burrow   *Fuller Smith & Turner - Brewers Handbook*

Bradley H W   1982 *A Handbook of Coins of the British Isles.*

Butler Margaret L   1989 *Barnes and Mortlake People in the Reign of Charles II.* Barnes and Mortlake History Society

Cockin Maurice S   1954 *Mortlake and her Church.* Privately Printed

Davis Ben   1981 *The Traditional English Pub, A way of Drinking.* The Architectural Press Ltd., London

Dunkling L and Wright G   1994 *Dictionary of Pub Names.* Wordsworth Editions Ltd

Gibson J and Hunter J   1994 *Victuallers' Licences. Records for Family and Local Historians.* Federation of Family History Societies

Glover B   1998 *The New Guide to Beer.* Anness Publishing Ltd

Hailstone C	1987	*Hammersmith Bridge.* Barnes and Mortlake History Society
Heselton K Y	1988	*A History of Sunbury's Pubs.* Sunbury and Shepperton Local History Society
Lilleywhite B	1972	*London Signs. A reference book of London Signs from earliest times to about the mid nineteenth century.* George Allen & Unwin Ltd
Linecar H	1971	*Coin and Medal Collecting for Pleasure and Profit.*
Martin A G	1974	*Inns and Taverns of Walton & Weybridge.* Walton and Weybridge Local History Society
Marshall Rose C	1961	*Nineteenth Century Mortlake and East Sheen.* Privately Printed
Monckton H A	1966	*A History of English Ale and Beer.* Bodley Head
Monckton H A	1982	*The Story of the British Pub.*
Sturley M	1990	*The Breweries and Public Houses of Guildford.* E & E Plumridge Ltd
Taylor John	1636	*Taverns in the Ten Shires Round London.*
Whichelow C	1998	*Pubs of Wimbledon Village (Past & Present).* Enigma Publishing
Wykes A		*Ale and Hearty.*

Index

Abbott, John 91
Abrahamson, Stephen Glen 35
Addison, Richard 144
Agate, William 110
Aldington, Robert George 122
Aldridge, S 133
ale conner 9, 10
ale houses 7, 9, 10, 11
ale-silver 9
ale stake 10
ale taster 9, 10
Alexandra, Rose Day 145
Alexandra, Princess of Wales 145
Alexandra, Queen 145
Allam, John 50
Alloway, Thomas Chas 127
Allsorp, S 132
Amos, Charles 65
Amos, William 65
Anderson, John Eustace 118, 125, 137
Angles, The 108
Archway Street 82
Arnell, J 70
Arnold, Dorothy 35
Ash family, The 17
Ash, R 88
Assize 9
Aubrey, Henry 112
Austin, P 35

Bacon, Charlotte Mrs 85
Bacon, Thomas 85
Bagley, Richard 62
Bagley's Stile 62
Bailey, Elizabeth Mrs 17
Bailey, Henry 96
Bailey, John 17
Bailey, Sidney V 34
Bainbridge, Anthony Fothergil 18
Baker, Mary Mrs 110
Baker, S 63
Balls, K L 65
Balls, Kenneth Leslie 141
Barker, Isabel 130
Barker, John 125

Barker, Sarah 125
Barn Elms 34
Barnes Borough Council 7, 78, 79, 97, 114
Barnes Bowling Club 38
Barnes Community Association 89
Barnes Churchwarden's 17, 18, 23, 36, 41
Barnes Cycling Club 23, 24
Barnes High Street 18, 23, 89, 90
Barnes Terrace 41, 43, 84
Barnes Tricycle Meet 31
Barnes Vestry 36, 110
Barnes Waterfront 88
Barr, Henry 17
Barr, Thomas 17
Barrett, Hubert Owen 133
Barrow, H A 82
Barry, Michael 63
Bass Taverns 77
Basse, William 142
Basten, Edward 90
Bazalgette, Sir Joseph 145
Beard, John 26
Beare, The 7, 10, 11, 93
bede-ale 9
Beehive, The 75
beer shop 11, 79
Bell, Jepe Nalder 55
Belsham, James 23
Bendel, James 31
Benevolent Brothers Friendly Society 70
Benham, Richard 124
Berkeley Hotel 96
betting shop 7
Beverley House 34
Biggs, Elizabeth Mrs 91
Biggs, John 36, 85, 124, 137, 146
Billingham, Jo 66
Birchmore, George 38
Bishop, Alexander Frederick 141
Bishop, Joseph 50
Bishop's Stortford 122
Bits about Barnes 43
Blacksmith Arms 157
Blackwell, John and Audrey 34
Blade, Mary Ann Mrs 76

Blade, Peter	76
Blake, Alexander Thomas	70
Blake, Ann	23
Blanchard, John	50
Bland, Edward	117
Blomfield, AW	97
Blue Anchor, The	142
Blundell, William	95
Boake, John	125
Boat Race Day	20
Boggia, Mary Ann	63
Boileau Arms, The	15, 34, 76-7, 146
Boileau, Charles Lestock	76
Boileau, Miss	108
Bone, James	76
Bosher, William	75
Bosley, Thomas	50
Bourn, Henry	142
Bourn, John	142
Bourne, Edgar	106
Bourne, Emily	106
Bourne, Henry	143
Bourne, Mike	10
Bourne, Philip	135
Boutelout, Peter	34
Bowles, George	38
Bowling, Mr	104
Bowyer, Henry	91
Boyne, W, Trade Tokens	157
Brady, William	62
Breach, John	114
Brewer, Alfred Horace	43
bride-ale	9
Bridge Hotel, The	15, 145
Bridge Road	31
Bridge, The	145
Brinkworth, Mary	139
Bristowe, A J	63
Brodie, H B	51
Brook, William	41
Brown, Ann Mrs	23
Brown, Frank	141
Brown, Samuel George	101
Brown, John	23
Brown, William	72
Browne, Thomas	95
Bubear, George	43
Bucknall, Martha	41
Budd, Leonard	138
Builders Arms, The	78
Bull, The	9, 54, 70, 95-100, 147
Bulls Head, The	17-20, 22, 43, 82, 88, 91
Bunten, Edward William	47
Burges, Robert	11
Burlton, William	62
Butcher, William	135
Butler, Eleanor M	138
Butler, Elizabeth Mrs	23
Butler, John	35
Butler, Philip 23	
Butler, Tim and Margaret	127
Butt, Henry Richard	122
Cackerill, Henry	41
Cafe More, The	79-81
Cafe Uno	91
Campaign for Real Ale	12
Cannon Brewery Company	31, 38-9
Carman, Edwin James	68
Carmen, Henry	135
Carpenter, Henry John	63
Castelnau	15, 31, 76
Castelnau de la Garde	76
Castelnau House	76
Castelnau Place	76
Castelnau Villas	76
Catalogue of Taverns	10
Cates, Charles H	20
Causeway, The	120
Cawdry, Thomas	139
Ceate, Samuel	50
Cedars Estate	104
Cedars, The	101
Census	10
Chalk, F	38
Challands Mr	41
Chambers, Martimus R	138
Charingbold, William	31
Charlie Butler, The	53, 61, 146
Charrington & Co Ltd	106
Chaucer Inns	76-7
Cheetcham, John	41
Chesefield, Albert Thomas	72
Christchurch Road	55

Christmas-ale 9
Church 7, 9, 18, 36
Church-ale 9
Church Commissioners 31
Church House 9, 142-3
Church Path 50, 114
Church records 9
Church Road 36
Churchill, A E 79
Churchill, Charles Joseph 141
City Arms/The Garter 158
Clarence Cottages 95
Clarence Row 95
Clark, William 41, 135
Clausen, Robbie and Jayne 102
Claydon, John 38
Clegg, Walter Edward 134
Clifford, John 55
Clipston's Beer House 79
Clipston, John Yeoman 79
Clowes, Mrs 41
Coach and Horses, The 23-5, 145
Coates, Henry 15
Cobbett, William 47
Coe, F H 51
Coe G F 51
Coe, Louisa Rose Mrs 79
Coffee House, The 36
Cole, Ernest 68
Coleman, W J 133
Coles Corner 41, 43, 84
Coles, John Albert 68
Collins, Frederick Shadrack 68
Collins, Henry 130
Collins, J F Mrs 68
Collins, Thomas 105
Cook, John 17-8, 41
Cook, Matthew 110
Cooper, H P 35
Cooper Leisure & Company, T G 68
Cooper, Mr 68
Cooper, T G 68
Cosham, James Edward 76
Coulston, Caroline Mrs 31
Coulston, Peter 31
Council meetings 9
Courage 28

Courage Barclay & Simonds Limited 68
Courage Brewery 26, 76
Court Rolls 23
court room 7
Courtice, Brian 85
Cowney, Christopher 50
Cowney, Mary Mrs 50
Cox, Edward 133
Cox, James 132
Cox, Samuel 132
Crane, William 65
Craston, Joseph Henry 47
Crew, Lucy Mrs 41
Crew, William 41
Cross Street 35
Crow, Mary Ann 85
Crow, John 85
Culverwell, James 38
Cunningham, Patrick Joseph 35

Dairy, John 62
Dale, George 114
D'Antraigues murder 41
Davies, Betsy Mrs 137
Davies, Rowland Alfred 132
Davies, S A Mrs 38
Davies, William 137
Davis, Mary Mrs 135
Davis, Sarah Ann Mrs 23
Davy, I K Mrs 75
Day, Edward 65
Day, George 132
Day, Henry 93
Dean and Chapter of St Paul's 43
Dean, Mr and Mrs 98
Dean, William 95
Dellar, Thomas 127
Dempsey, Edward 61
Denby, John 65
Derby Arms, The 56, 101-2, 147
Derby, Earl of 101
dicing 11
Dietrich, Anton Carl Heinrick Gustave 138
Dipper, Mr 120
Dixon, Mrs 55
Dixon, Thomas 55, 117
Dog Gate, The 118

Dog, The	118
Dogge, The	7, 118
Downing, Thomas	95
Dudding, G R	85
Dunkley's Field	118
Durham, Walter	130
Eagles, John	132
Easter-ale	9
Easter, Walter	96
Eastwood, Stephen	31
Ecclesiastical Commissioners	43
Edinburgh Castle, The	82-3, 146
Edmonds, B	122
Edmonds, Elizabeth Mrs	122
Edmonds, Miss	135
Edn Weatherstone & Co Ltd, Messrs	141
Edward, Thomas	26
Edwards, Iames	157
Edwards, Reginald Haspur	117
Edwards, Richard	54
Edwards, Susanna Mary	137
Elcock, Henry	135
Elcock, Susannah Mrs	135
Eleventh Regiment of Light Dragoons	50, 62, 70, 95, 125, 132, 135, 140
Elizabeth I,	156
Elliot, Robert	17-8
Ellis, George	101
Elson, David	125
Emberton, John	17
Emmerton, Thomas	157
Emnett, S A	23
Endersby, Arthur	47
Endersby, Frederick Ernest	47
Enfranchisement, Deed of	26
Englefield, George	132
English Heritage	39, 56
Entire	122
Everson, C	23
Everson, Frances Magdelene Mrs	23
Everson, John	23
Express Hotel, The	122
Fairall, George Thomas	141
Fairall, Theresa	141
Farnell, Watson	85, 111-2
Fenge, Ted	101
Ffitzwater, Ann Mrs	131
Ffitzwater, Edward	131
Ffitzwater, Richard	131
Ffunnel, Adam	139
Field, Charlotte Mrs	127
Field, Fanny and Eliza	67
Field, Frances	62
Field, James	63
Field, Mary	62
Firman, J E , Mr and Mrs	112
Firmston, John	65, 125, 137
Fisher, Charles	96
Fisher, John	91
Fisher, John and Julie	39
Fisher, L P D Mr	39
Fitchett, William Peter	138
Fitzgerald, Kean	125
Fitzgerald, Thomas	125
Five Alls, The	104
Flemming, Dan and Liz	20
Fletcher, Thomas	143
Flinn, Christopher	139
Foster, Eliza Mrs	65
Foster, Olivette Rose Mrs	72
Foster, Richard Davis	65
Friary Meux	83
Friel, John	34
Fuhr, Henry Charles	138
Fuller, Smith and Turner	11, 34, 125
Fuller, William	32
Gallagher, Stephen	61
gambling	11
Gamsey, John Canen	141
Garden House, The	77
Garraway Coffee House	41, 135
Garrett, George	20
Garter, W	96
Garter, Ye	120
Gatwood, Samuel	36
Gay, Robert	82
George III,	41, 132
Gibbons, Grinling	144
Gibson, Marjory	89
Glascock, Richard	118
Globe Theatre	142

Goddard, William 36
Godfrey, Francis Richard 137
Goff, Thomas 23
Goodwin, Charles 93, 157
Goolden, Edwin Richardson 20, 38
Gouldsmith, Thomas 95
Grand Metropolitan 54, 65, 72
Grand Metropolitan Estates 102
Granger, Lynne 28
Granger, Mr 30
Gratton, John 50
Gray, William 70
Green, A 122
Green, Thomas George 91
Greene King Plc 66
Greene, Percival John 47
Griffen, James 91
Griffiths, Martha Mrs 31
Grimshaw, James 62
Grombs, Robert 70
Groome, James William 63
Guildford 83
Gurr, Elizabeth 95
Gurr, Thomas 95

Hagger, Elizabeth Mrs 96
Hagger, Joseph W 96
Hailstone, Charles 54
Halford & Co, Messrs 70, 140
Halford, Elizabeth Streater 95
Halford and Topham, Messrs 70, 95
Halford and Weatherstone 95
Halfway House, The 26, 145
Hall, Aaron Lambert 95
Hall, Isaac 70
Hall, John 18, 55
Hall, W J 133
Hall and Woodhouse Limited 68
Hammersmith Bridge 15, 20, 76, 96, 145
Hammersmith Bridge Road 79
Hammond, Elizabeth Mrs 95
Hammond, John 70, 95
Hammond, John Rd 50
Hammond, Robert 31
Hampton Square 114
Hand and Flower, The 105
Hanks, Jonadab 141

Harding, K 38
Harding, Mr 62
Harding, Thomas James 127
Hardwick, Dance and Couse 36
Hare and Hounds, The 7, 50-3, 118, 145
Harris, Len 39
Harrison, John 41
Hartley, Timothy 157
Hartnell, Harry Symonds 101
Hart's Horn, The 142
Harvey, Charles 114
Harvey, Len 101
Harwood, Arthur Edward Victor 134
Hawkes & Co 122
Hayden, Harriet Mrs 23
Hayes, Joseph 114
Head, John 91
Heal, Francis 131
Henden, Charles Frederick 141
Henden, Jessie Maud Mrs 141
Herald, The 122
Hester, Jane 114
Higgs, A J 63
Higham, Charles 55
Hill, E J 75
Hill, Henry 91
Hill, Richard 93
Hill, Thomas 38, 70
Hill, William 91
Hitchings, William 36
Hoare, John 135, 137
Hodge, E J T 133
Hodgsons Brewery 28
Hodgson's Kingston Brewery Co Ltd 117
Holden, Mr 120
Holden, Dorothy Mrs 120
Holden, Susannah 131
Holloway, Frederick C Robert 63
Holmes, James 117
Holt, Reginald 75
Holyard, James 50
Hope, The 122
Hopperton, L C G 68
Horan, Terry 106
Hornes, Percy James 117
Hornes, The 143
Hornsby, Elizabeth Mrs 23

Hornsby, Francis 23
Houseman, Soloman 76
Howard, J William 63
Howell, George 70
Hulbert, J 38
Hulbert, John 18
Hunt, Elizabeth 17
Hunt, Henry 17, 41
Huntley, Henry Francis 130
Huntsman, William 138
Hurley, Patrick 138
Hutchinson, W J 81

Ind Coope Ltd 39, 83
Ingram, Thomas Frederick 63
Isaac, Arthur 55
Issenburg, Peter 11

Jackman, George 122
Jackman, Thomas 105
Jackson, Alexander H 38
Jacobs, Elizabeth Mrs 131
Jacobs, William 131
James I, ...156
jazz music 20
Jefferies, L S 28
Jellett, Henry 141
Jemmett, Charles 41
Jenkins, John 125
Jennings, Alfred 130
Johnson, H M 56
Johnson, Harold 117
Johnson, John 108
Jolly Gardeners, The 26, 62-3, 139, 146
Jolly Maltman, The 124
Jolly Milkman, The 65-6, 126, 146
Jones, George Jesse 142
Jones, Peggy Mrs 56
Justices of the Peace 10

Kelly, John 138
Kelsey, Thomas 23
Kempson, George Streater 95
Kempson and Topham 95
Kerfhaw, Jof 125
Kerfoot, Thomas 26
Kettley, R H 110

Kew Bridge 122
Kings Arms, The 7, 11, 63, 65, 84,
....125-6, 130, 137
Kings Head, The 17, 88, 144
Kinsley, Joseph H 72
Kisby, Edward 65
Knapp, Joseph 125
Knight, George Sidney 23
Knight, Sarah Ann Mrs 23
Knowland Bros 130
Koklhausen, J W 51
Kolmar, David 113
Kolmar, Maggie 113

Land, Eddie 140
Land Tax Records 17, 125
Langridge, George 135
Larkin, Samuel 70
Lashman, L G 63
Lavonsky, Emanuel 91
Lawn, John 79
Leaver, John 131
Leigh, Edith Maud Mrs 38
Levett, Arthur 91
Lewis, John 120
Licensed Victuallers Recognizances 17, 23, 95,
....125, 140
Lindsey, Charles 106
Lipscombe, Matthew 124
Littlewood, Jas George 112
Llewellyn, Mary Ann 34
Lockwood, John Henry 47
Lodge Avenue 110
London Brewery 142
Longman, Frederick 65
Lonsdale Road 17, 76, 91
Lord Napier, The 127-9, 147
Lord of the Manor 7, 43, 79, 90
Lorton, John 95
Lovett, Emily 105
Lower Richmond Road ...62, 65, 70, 126, 138-9
Lucus, Edwin 72
Lund, Samuel 135

Maggot and Maybe, The 87
Magic Pub Company, The 65-6
Maidenhead, The 7, 10, 142-3

Malthouse Passage 18
Mander, John 139
Manor Arms, The 28-30
Mapleden, William 41
Marfleet, E F 23
Marfleet, Frank 23
Marfleet, S A Mrs 23
Market Gardener, The 85-7, 146
Marnane, David Paul 77
Marriner, Graham 65
Marriner, Margaret Mrs 65
Martiell, Alice Mrs 70
Martin, Alice Mrs 41
Martin, John 41
Martin, William 132
Mason, S Mrs 91
Mason, Thomas 91
Matthews, J 23
Mayoral chair 97
Mc Cormack, Sean 97
McKellar, Nederick 78
Mecca Speciality Leisure 98
Medworth, Joseph 50
Merchant Taylor Arms, The 157
Messit, Karen Mrs 25
Meux's Brewery Company Ltd 82
Miller, Ann 91
Millsum, Edward 23
Moff, Peter 140
Moff, Sarah Mrs 140
Mollett, B 23
Monk, Richard Crowdy 43
Moore, Tom 23
Morris, W 96
Morrison, Deny Edward 47
Mortlake and Barnes Guardian 31
Mortlake Brewery 95, 122
Mortlake District Highway Board 50
Mortlake Green 70
Mortlake High Street 53, 61-2, 122, 124, 127,
.... 130-1, 137, 140, 142
Mortlake Hotel, The 130
Mortlake Street 62, 131
Mortlake Waterfront 135
Morton, Noel 35
Muir, Bill 54
Murrell, T A 106

Murphy, Pat and Linda 127-8
Nalton, Mary 137
Nantes, Edict of 76
Naylor, Eric Hunter 47
Newall, Edna 113
Newall, John 113
Newman, Charles 51
Newton, C S 34
Newton, Eliza Mrs 110
Newton, Robert 125
Nicholls, John 41
North Barnes Residents Association 77
North London Tricycle Club 31
North Surrey Bicycle Association 82

O'Brien, Joseph Michael 117
O'Connell, Rory 83
O'Donovan, Brian 56
Odd Fellows Lodge 63, 126
Old George Passage 134
Old George, The 61, 131-4, 140, 143
Old Rangoon, The 77
Ommanney, Col 118
Orchin, George 132
Order of Council 10
Otley, Katherine Jane Mrs 51
Owen, Robert 113
Oxford and Cambridge Boat Race 31, 47

Packwood, William 76
Padgett, William 31
Pale Lane 118
Palewell Lodge 50
Pankhurst, Henry 18
Parish Accounts 18
Parish Boundaries 18
Parker, Charles 70
Parker, William John 63
Parson, G W 127
Parsons, Emma Mrs 62
Parsons, J 62
Pearce, T P 63
Penketh, Richard Joseph 133
Penrhyn, Charlotte Lady 101
Penrhyn Cresent 104
Penrhyn, E Hugh Leycester 104

Penrhyn Rooms 97
Penston, Ann Mrs 85
Perkins, Harold 56
Perkins, Peggy Mrs 56
Perkins, Wendy Mrs 61
Perrin, Arthur S 61
Phillips, Anne Mrs 125
Phillips, Augustine 142
Phillips, Charles Henry 26
Phillips, Richard 26, 91
Phillips, Samuel 70
Phillips and Co 141
Phillips and Wigan, Messrs 70, 72, 96, 141
Pickled Newt, The 65, 147
Pig and Whistle, The 54, 145-6
Pike, Christopher 38
Pike, Richard 70
Plough, The 50, 117, 146
Plough and Harrow, The 51, 55
Plow, Thomas 118
Pocock, Charlotte 127
Pocock, George 127
Pocock, Joseph 26
Porter, Anne Mrs 26
Porter, Joseph 26
Porter, Samuel 26
Potter, Alfred 75
Potter, Dorothy Alice 101
Potter, Thomas Charles 101
Potter, Thomas 142
Powell, Thomas 50
Preble, William 62
Preston, Elizabeth Mrs 17
Price, Gwendolyn Barbara Mrs 134
Price, James 125, 134
Price, Thomas 125, 134
Priest Bridge 26, 85, 118
Prince, Edward 141
Princess Arms, The 7, 10
Princes Road 106, 110
Prior, John 62
Pugh, Frederick 141
Pugh, William James Frederick 141

Quarter Sessions 36
Queens Arms, The 106, 147
Queen's Head Court 135

Queens Head, The 65, 68, 126, 135-8
Queen's Messenger 18
Queens Road 105, 108, 110

Railway Arms, The 79-81
Railway Hotel, The 79-81
Railway Side 28, 75
Railway Street 78
Railway Tavern, The 68, 146
Ram Brewery 134
Rayne Deer, The 88
Red Lion, The 31-34
Red Rover, The 79-81, 146
Reeve, Thomas 88
Reynolds, Thomas 76
Richards, Florence Mrs 117
Richards, Jean and Keith 63
Richards, William Walter 23
Richardson, John 95
Richardson, Joseph 110
Richmond Conveyance Company 125
Richmond Council 39, 106, 128
Richmond Herald 34
Richmond Informer 102
Richmond Magistrates 114
Richmond Park 111
Richmond, William 62
Riley, H A 117
Rising Sun, The 36
Roberts, Percy F 138
Roberts, Robert 50
Robinson, John 17
Rochford, Ellen Miss 85, 87
Rock Avenue 110
Rock's Lane 110
Roehampton Road 79
Rogers, James 70
Rollo, Andrew 82
Rollo, Charlotte Eliza 89
Rose, The 89
Rose House 89
Rose of Denmark, The 35, 145
Rowson, George 114
Royal Academy 97
Royal Brewery (Brentford) Ltd 68
Royal Opera House, The 61
Royal, William 36

Royall Garter, Ye 120
Rudkin, Bessie 55
Ruffell, George Richard 75
Russell, A E 76
Russell, Thomas 125
Russet, John 131

St Marys Church 7
Saddler, William 90
Sale of Beer Act 11
Sampson, Bishop 110
Saunders, John 131
Saunders, Mary Mrs 131
Saunders, Sarah Mrs 131
Saunders, William 131
scot-ale 9
Scott, John, Dr 108
Scott, Mr 137
Scott, Mary Mrs 137
Scottish and Newcastle 65, 72
Scottish and Newcastle Retail 15, 54
Scryver, John 11
Sell, Stewart 47
Sewell, George Edward 31
Seymour, Joseph 23
Sharp, George 72
Sharp, John 55
Sharp, Louisa 55
Sharpe, Paul 65
Shearman, George E 34
Sheen Common 111
Sheen Gate 118
Sheen Gate Gardens 104
Sheen Green 118
Sheen Lane 53-4, 68, 95-6, 103, 114, 118
Shene 99
Ship Hotel, The 70-2, 142-3, 146
Ship Lane 62, 70, 142
Shovel at Barnes, The 157
Sim, John 55
Simmonds, William G 51
Sims, Mrs 135
Singer, Edmond 17
Singer, James 17
Slater, James Henry 82
Smith Elizabeth 125
Smith, Mr 41

Smith, James 63
Smith, Joseph 125
Smith, John 17, 70
Smith, Thomas 125
Smith, William 41, 55
Smith, William Looke 20
Souster, John 36
Souster, Thomas 23, 141
South London Tricycle Club 31
South Worple Way 108
Southwark 10, 142
Spencer, Earl 26
sports centre 7
Spur Bridge 108
Spur, The 108, 110, 147
Squibb & Son 135
Squire, John 141
Stable Bistro, The 20
Stag Brewery, The 15
Stanley, Edward, Earl of Derby 101
Stanley Road 101
Star and Garter, The 120
St Ann's Passage 78
Stevens, Arthur, Major General 18
Stibbing, Richard 23
Stillwell, Stephen 62
Stokes, John 36
Stone, Frederick 55
Stone, Stephen 117
Stove, Thomas 131
Stort Navigation Canal 122
Strugglers, The 31
Sumner, William 141
Sun, The 7, 36, 145
Sun Coffee House, The 36
Sun Inn, The 36-9
Swaine, William 76
Swinyard, W L 63

Tancock, Gwendoline Mrs 127
Tapestry Alley 135
Tapestry Court 135
Tapestry Works 135
Taverns in the Ten Shires around London 10, 143
Taylor, Buck and Pauline 81
Taylor, John 10, 125, 143
Taylor, Samuel 125

Taylor Walker Ltd	39
Taylor, William	125
Terrace, The	41, 82
Tew, William	137
Thames Bank	70, 120
Thames Street	62, 125
Thompson and Dempsey Limited	61
Thompson, Michael and Jill	26
Thornton, George	141
Thornton, James	18, 41
Thornton, Mr	141
Thornton, Thomas M	141
Thornton, William	157
Thorpe, Benjamin	82
Three Cups Tavern, The	90
Three Tuns, The	62, 139
Tiernan, Paul and Tracy	128
Tithe Commissioners	36
Tokens	156-8
Tolley, Albert	20
Tooley, William	20
Toten, Joseph	41, 43
Tower House	76
Towler, Robert Thomas	101
Tree House, The	83
Trehorne Road	110
Trevy, Charles	41
Trevy, Elizabeth	41
Trevy, John	41
Trevy, William	41
Tritton, George	62
Tucker, Phoebe	10, 143
Turner, Dennis Victor	51, 53
Turner, E Mrs	112
Turner, George	111-2
Turner, Ian and Mary	61
Turner, Victor	51
Turner, William	111
Two Brewers, The	140-1
Twogood, George	70
Twogood, Thomas	70
Ullathorne, Norman	87
Upper Bridge Road	15
Upper Richmond Road	79, 120
Upper Richmond Road West	50, 57, 93, 95-6, 101, 104
Venner, Mr	114
Venner, Mrs	114
vestry meeting	31
vestry meetings	7
Vestry Minute Books	10
Vestry Minutes, Barnes	17
Victoria, The	111-3, 147
village constables	10
Wagnell, Charles	38
Waite, Melvin	66
Wakefield, Thomas	41
Waldo, Mary Scott	23
Walker, Mr	41
Walker, William	18
Wallingers	140
Ward, Charles Edward	72
Ward, Peter Matthew	141
Wardell, Gilbert	15
Ware, George	122
Waring, (nee Hunt) Frances	17
Waring, John	11, 17-8, 23, 50
Waring, John Edward	36, 132
Waring, Mary Catherine	18
Waring, Mary	50
Warner, Charles	84
Warner Family	41
Warner, Robert	120
Warren, Sarah Mrs	18
Warwick, E G B	51
Warwick, Edward George	101
Waterman	10, 91, 137, 142-3
Watermans Arms, The	18, 20, 91
Watney	65, 85, 97, 117, 130
Watney & Co	72, 96, 101, 110, 113, 130, 138, 141
Watney, Combe Reid & Co	15, 78-9, 99, 127, 141
Watney Mann Ltd	141
Watneys Brewery	128, 131
Watson, Jane	17
Watson, Paul	17
Watson, William	17
Wayside	108
Webb, Isabel	130
Webb, Phyllis Mrs	75

Webb, Sheila 26
Wederall, Ernest Edward 141
Well Lane 55
Wellington, Duke of 11
West End 126
Westby, Frank 56
Westby, Philomena Mrs 56
West Fulham League 35
West London Sketch 43
West Temple Sheen 111
Westfield House 82
Wheatley 68
Wheatley, George Turner 68
Wheatsheaf, The 55, 114-7
Whitbread London Ltd 26
White Hart Hotel, Ye 18, 41-7, 84, 127, 145
White Hart Lane 82, 84
White Horse, The 36
White, Mrs 120
White, Peter 120, 158
White, Walter George 138
Whitehead, Frank 72
Whitsun-ale 9
Whittick, Henry 31
Whitworth Arms, The 142
Wigan, James 123
Wilcox, Christopher 43
Wilcox, Tom 43
Wilde, William John 110
Willes, Symon 142
Williams, C W 31
Williams, D 15
Williams, Edith Mrs 15
Williams, Henry 15
Williams, John 11
Williams, N L 68
Williams, Percy 15
Williams and Young 31
Williamson, G C 157
Wimble, John 23
Wimbledon Court Rolls 139
Wimbledon, Manor of 26
Winch, Alfred William 43
Wood, Frederick John 117
Wood, John James 65
Wood, William 135
Woodiss, Ralph 50

Workhouse, new 17
Wright, Benjamin Thomas 90
Wright, C 35
Wright, Cathy Mrs 110
Wright, Thomas 41
Wyatt, John 131-2
Wynn, Charles Henry 79

Yates, Letitia 17
Yates, Margaret Mrs 17
Yates, William 17
Young and Bainbridge 23, 38, 50, 62, 132
Young & Co 50-1, 61, 133-4, 146
Young, C A 43
Young, Charles Florence 18, 43
Young, Elizabeth 43
Young, Mary Ann 43
Young's Brewery 62